GREAT

JOBS

FOR

Art
Majors

Blythe Camenson

VGM Career Books

Chicago   New York   San Francisco   Lisbon   London   Madrid   Mexico City
Milan   New Delhi   San Juan   Seoul   Singapore   Sydney   Toronto

Library of Congress Cataloging-in-Publication Data

Camenson, Blythe.
      Great jobs for art majors / Blythe Camenson. — 2nd ed.
          p.   cm. — (Great jobs for)
      Includes bibliographical references and index.
      ISBN 0-07-140903-3 (alk. paper)
      1. Art—Vocational guidance—United States.   I. Title.   II. Series.

  N6505 .C33   2003
  702'.3'73—dc21   2002035747

1 2 3 4 5 6 7 8 9 0 DOC/DOC 2 1 0 9 8 7 6 5 4 3

ISBN 0-07-140903-3

McGraw-Hill books are available at special quantity discounts to use as premiums and sales promotions, or for use in corporate training programs. For more information, please write to the Director of Special Sales, Professional Publishing, McGraw-Hill, Two Penn Plaza, New York, NY 10121-2298. Or contact your local bookstore.

This book is printed on acid-free paper.

With much love and admiration to Dwina Murphy-Gibb,
the most creative soul I know.

Contents

Acknowledgments

James Anderson, stained glass artist; Anderson Stained Glass, Boston
Patricia Baker, costumer; Plimoth Plantation, Plymouth, Massachusetts
Matthew Carone, owner; Carone Art Gallery, Fort Lauderdale, Florida
Aileen Chuk, associate registrar; Registrar's Office, Metropolitan Museum
of Art, New York
Joan Gardner, chief conservator; Carnegie Museum of Natural History,
Pittsburgh
Tom Gebherdt, cooper; Plimoth Plantation, Plymouth, Massachusetts
Erica Hirshler, assistant curator; Paintings Department, Museum of Fine
Arts, Boston
Deb Mason, potter; Plimoth Plantation, Plymouth, Massachusetts
Peggy Peters, art educator; San Antonio, Texas
Joel Pontz, artisan; Plimoth Plantation, Plymouth, Massachusetts
Lynne Robbins, art educator; Boston

Introduction

Humankind has been expressing itself through art since the beginning of recorded history. The need to create and to share those creations has been an all-consuming force that even time has not suppressed.

Early cave paintings suggest a collaborative effort: for each clan artist (except for the first) there must have been a teacher, a mentor, and a clan historian, the storyteller passing on significant events from one generation to another. Perhaps even a color and design expert was there, to discuss pigment and the most aesthetic placement of drawings upon the walls.

The image of the starving artist painting alone in his garret belies the fact that today, the collaboration continues. Artists study and are influenced by those who came before them. Art historians, delve into the art of past and more recent cultures then pass that knowledge on through their writings and teachings. Art educators also contribute by teaching budding artists the time-tested techniques and methods for creating art.

Even the art critic adds to the collaborative effort, albeit inadvertently, helping to shape public tastes with his opinions. The museum curator or art gallery owner furthers the cause, choosing which art to display, which artist to promote.

Although many think of the creation of art as a solo affair, art does not stand alone. It functions in its own ecosystem, as strong as the water we drink and the air we breathe. Each component has its place, and to continue to exist, all components must be present.

Where you, the art major, can fit into this system, is an individual choice based on your interests, skills, and desires. Within these pages you will learn about the variety of settings in which an artist can work and the corresponding job titles.

PART ONE

THE JOB SEARCH

I

The Self-Assessment

Self-assessment is the process by which you begin to acknowledge your own particular blend of education, experiences, values, needs, and goals. It provides the foundation for career planning and the entire job search process. Self-assessment involves looking inward and asking yourself what can sometimes prove to be difficult questions. This self-examination should lead to an intimate understanding of your personal traits, your personal values, your consumption patterns and economic needs, your longer-term goals, your skill base, your preferred skills, and your underdeveloped skills.

You come to the self-assessment process knowing yourself well in some of these areas, but you may still be uncertain about other aspects. You may be well aware of your consumption patterns, but have you spent much time specifically identifying your longer-term goals or your personal values as they relate to work? No matter what level of self-assessment you have undertaken to date, it is now time to clarify all of these issues and questions as they relate to the job search.

The knowledge you gain in the self-assessment process will guide the rest of your job search. In this book, you will learn about all of the following tasks:

- Writing résumés and cover letters
- Researching careers and networking
- Interviewing and job offer considerations

In each of these steps, you will rely on and often return to the understanding gained through your self-assessment. Any individual seeking employment must be able and willing to express these facets of his or her personality to recruiters and interviewers throughout the job search. This communication allows you to show the world who you are so that together with employers you can determine whether there will be a workable match with a given job or career path.

How to Conduct a Self-Assessment

The self-assessment process goes on naturally all the time. People ask you to clarify what you mean, you make a purchasing decision, or you begin a new relationship. You react to the world and the world reacts to you. How you understand these interactions and any changes you might make because of them are part of the natural process of self-discovery. There is, however, a more comprehensive and efficient way to approach self-assessment with regard to employment.

Because self-assessment can become a complex exercise, we have distilled it into a seven-step process that provides an effective basis for undertaking a job search. The seven steps include the following:

1. Understanding your personal traits
2. Identifying your personal values
3. Calculating your economic needs
4. Exploring your longer-term goals
5. Enumerating your skill base
6. Recognizing your preferred skills
7. Assessing skills needing further development

As you work through your self-assessment, you might want to create a worksheet similar to the one shown in Exhibit 1.1, starting on the following page. Or you might want to keep a journal of the thoughts you have as you undergo this process. There will be many opportunities to revise your self-assessment as you start down the path of seeking a career.

Step 1   Understanding Your Personal Traits

Each person has a unique personality that he or she brings to the job search process. Gaining a better understanding of your personal traits can help you evaluate job and career choices. Identifying these traits and then finding employment that allows you to draw on at least some of them can create a rewarding and fulfilling work experience. If potential employment doesn't allow you to use these preferred traits, it is important to decide whether you

Exhibit 1.1
SELF-ASSESSMENT WORKSHEET

Step 1. Understand Your Personal Traits
  The personal traits that describe me are:
  (Include all of the words that describe you.)
  The ten personal traits that most accurately describe me are:
  (List these ten traits.)

Step 2. Identify Your Personal Values
  Working conditions that are important to me include:
  (List working conditions that would have to exist for you to accept a position.)
  The values that go along with my working conditions are:
  (Write down the values that correspond to each working condition.)
  Some additional values I've decided to include are:
  (List those values you identify as you conduct this job search.)

Step 3. Calculate Your Economic Needs
  My estimated minimum annual salary requirement is:
  (Write the salary you have calculated based on your budget.)
  Starting salaries for the positions I'm considering are:
  (List the name of each job you are considering and the associated starting salary.)

Step 4. Explore Your Longer-Term Goals
  My thoughts on longer-term goals right now are:
  (Jot down some of your longer-term goals as you know them right now.)

Step 5. Enumerate Your Skill Base
  The general skills I possess are:
  (List the skills that underlie tasks you are able to complete.)
  The specific skills I possess are:
  (List more technical or specific skills that you possess, and indicate your level of expertise.)
  General and specific skills that I want to promote to employers for the jobs I'm considering are:
  (List general and specific skills for each type of job you are considering.)

continued

Step 6. Recognize Your Preferred Skills

Skills that I would like to use on the job include:

(List skills that you hope to use on the job, and indicate how often you'd like to use them.)

Step 7. Assess Skills Needing Further Development

Some skills that I'll need to acquire for the jobs I'm considering include:

(Write down skills listed in job advertisements or job descriptions that you don't currently possess.)

I believe I can build these skills by:

(Describe how you plan to acquire these skills.)

can find other ways to express them or whether you would be better off not considering this type of job. Interests and hobbies pursued outside of work hours can be one way to use personal traits you don't have an opportunity to draw on in your work. For example, if you consider yourself an outgoing person and the kinds of jobs you are examining allow little contact with other people, you may be able to achieve the level of interaction that is comfortable for you outside of your work setting. If such a compromise seems impractical or otherwise unsatisfactory, you probably should explore only jobs that provide the interaction you want and need on the job.

Many young adults who are not very confident about their employability will downplay their need for income. They will say, "Money is not all that important if I love my work." But if you begin to document exactly what you need for housing, transportation, insurance, clothing, food, and utilities, you will begin to understand that some jobs cannot meet your financial needs and it doesn't matter how wonderful the job is. If you have to worry each payday about bills and other financial obligations, you won't be very effective on the job. Begin now to be honest with yourself about your needs.

Begin the self-assessment process by creating an inventory of your personal traits. Make a list of as many words as possible to describe yourself. Words like *accurate, creative, future-oriented, relaxed,* or *structured* are just a few examples. In addition, you might ask people who know you well how they might describe you.

Focusing on Selected Personal Traits. Of all the traits you identified, select the ten you believe most accurately describe you. Keep track of these ten traits.

Considering Your Personal Traits in the Job Search Process. As you begin exploring jobs and careers, watch for matches between your personal traits and the job descriptions you read. Some jobs will require many personal traits you know you possess, and others will not seem to match those traits.

Working as an art teacher, for example, will draw upon your reserves of creativity—but not necessarily for your own work. Teaching is essentially outer-directed, and your ability to create methods to stimulate, encourage, and guide students will be far more important than your own attention to technique and color. Teaching calls for the ability to motivate others and to support their efforts without being overly critical or judgmental. Art teachers, especially those working within a school system, must be sensitive to the needs and goals of their students while meeting the criteria set by others.

Your ability to respond to changing conditions, your decision-making ability, productivity, creativity, and verbal skills all have a bearing on your success in and enjoyment of your work life. To better guarantee success, be sure to take the time needed to understand these traits in yourself.

Step 2   Identifying Your Personal Values

Your personal values affect every aspect of your life, including employment, and they develop and change as you move through life. Values can be defined as principles that we hold in high regard, qualities that are important and desirable to us. Some values aren't ordinarily connected to work (love, beauty, color, light, relationships, family, or religion), and others are (autonomy, cooperation, effectiveness, achievement, knowledge, and security). Our values determine, in part, the level of satisfaction we feel in a particular job.

Defining Acceptable Working Conditions. One facet of employment is the set of working conditions that must exist for someone to consider taking a job.

Each of us would probably create a unique list of acceptable working conditions, but items that might be included on many people's lists are the amount of money you would need to be paid, how far you are willing to drive or travel, the amount of freedom you want in determining your own schedule, whether you would be working with people or data or things, and the types of tasks you would be willing to do. Your conditions might include statements of working conditions you will *not* accept; for example, you might not be willing to work at night or on weekends or holidays.

If you were offered a job tomorrow, what conditions would have to exist for you to realistically consider accepting the position? Take some time and make a list of these conditions.

Realizing Associated Values. Your list of working conditions can be used to create an inventory of your values relating to jobs and careers you are exploring. For example, if one of your conditions stated that you wanted to earn at least $30,000 per year, the associated value would be financial gain. If another condition was that you wanted to work with a friendly group of people, the value that went along with that might be belonging or interaction with people.

Relating Your Values to the World of Work. As you read the job descriptions you come across either in this book, in newspapers and magazines, or online, think about the values associated with each position.

For example, a curator in an art museum is responsible for the preservation of the collection and for implementing its visual accessibility to the public. Associated values are precision, effectiveness, and community.

At least some of the associated values in the field you're exploring should match those you extracted from your list of working conditions. Take a second look at any values that don't match up. How important are they to you? What will happen if they are not satisfied on the job? Can you incorporate those personal values elsewhere? Your answers need to be brutally honest. As you continue your exploration, be sure to add to your list any additional values that occur to you.

Step 3   Calculating Your Economic Needs

Each of us grew up in an environment that provided for certain basic needs, such as food and shelter, and, to varying degrees, other needs that we now consider basic, such as cable television, E-mail, or an automobile. Needs such as privacy, space, and quiet, which at first glance may not appear to be monetary needs, may add to housing expenses and so should be considered as you examine your economic needs. For example, if you place a high value on a large, open living space for yourself, it would be difficult to satisfy that need without an associated high housing cost, especially in a densely populated city environment.

As you prepare to move into the world of work and become responsible for meeting your own basic needs, it is important to consider the salary you will need to be able to afford a satisfying standard of living. The three-step process outlined here will help you plan a budget, which in turn will allow you to evaluate the various career choices and geographic locations you are considering. The steps include (1) developing a realistic budget, (2) examining starting salaries, and (3) using a cost-of-living index.

Developing a Realistic Budget. Each of us has certain expectations for the kind of lifestyle we want to maintain. To begin the process of defining your economic needs, it will be helpful to determine what you expect to spend on routine monthly expenses. These expenses include housing, food, transportation, entertainment, utilities, loan repayments, and revolving charge accounts. You may not currently spend anything for certain items, but you probably will have to once you begin supporting yourself. As you develop this budget, be generous in your estimates, but keep in mind any items that could be reduced or eliminated. If you are not sure about the cost of a certain item, talk with family or friends who would be able to give you a realistic estimate.

If this is new or difficult for you, start to keep a log of expenses right now. You may be surprised at how much you actually spend each month for food or stamps or magazines. Household expenses and personal grooming items can often loom very large in a budget, as can auto repairs or home maintenance.

Income taxes must also be taken into consideration when examining salary requirements. State and local taxes vary, so it is difficult to calculate exactly the effect of taxes on the amount of income you need to generate. To roughly estimate the gross income necessary to generate your minimum annual salary requirement, multiply the minimum salary you have calculated by a factor of 1.35. The resulting figure will be an approximation of what your gross income would need to be, given your estimated expenses.

Examining Starting Salaries. Starting salaries for each of the career tracks are provided throughout this book. These salary figures can be used in conjunction with the cost-of-living index (discussed in the next section) to determine whether you would be able to meet your basic economic needs in a given geographic location.

Using a Cost-of-Living Index. If you are thinking about trying to get a job in a geographic region other than the one where you now live, understanding differences in the cost of living will help you come to a more informed decision about making a move. By using a cost-of-living index, you can compare salaries offered and the cost of living in different locations with what you know about the salaries offered and the cost of living in your present location.

Many variables are used to calculate the cost-of-living index. Often included are housing, groceries, utilities, transportation, health care, clothing, and entertainment expenses. Right now you do not need to worry about the details associated with calculating a given index. The main purpose of this exercise is to help you understand that pay ranges for entry-level positions may not vary greatly, but the cost of living in different locations *can* vary tremendously.

If you lived in Cleveland, Ohio, for example, and you were interested in working as an assistant registrar for a small art museum, you would earn, on average, $26,000 annually. But let's say you're also thinking about moving to New York, Los Angeles, or Denver. You know you can live on $26,000 in Cleveland, but you want to be able to equate that salary in other locations you're considering. How much will you need to earn in those locations to do this? Figuring the cost of living for each city will show you.

Let's walk through this example. In any cost-of-living index, the number 100 represents the national average, and each city is assigned an index number based on current prices in that city for items included in the index (housing, food, and so forth). In the index we used for the table that follows, New York was assigned the number 213.3, Los Angeles's index was 124.6, Denver's was 100.0, and Cleveland's index was 114.3. In other words, it costs more than twice as much to live in New York as it does in Denver. We can set up a table to determine exactly how much you would have to earn in each of these cities to have the same buying power that you have in Cleveland.

You would have to earn $48,519 in New York, $28,342 in Los Angeles, and $22,747 in Denver to match the buying power of $26,000 in Cleveland.

JOB: ASSISTANT REGISTRAR

City	Index	Equivalent Salary
New York	213.3	
		× $26,000 = $48,519 in New York
Cleveland	114.3	
Los Angeles	124.6	
		× $26,000 = $28,342 in Los Angeles
Cleveland	114.3	
Denver	100.0	
		× $26,000 = $22,747 in Denver
Cleveland	114.3	

If you would like to determine whether it's financially worthwhile to make any of these moves, one more piece of information is needed: the salaries of assistant registrars in these other cities.

If you moved to New York and secured employment as an assistant registrar in an art museum, you would not be able to maintain a lifestyle similar to the one you led in Cleveland; in fact, you would have to add more than 50 percent to your income to maintain a similar lifestyle in New York. The same would not be true for a move to Los Angeles or Denver. You would increase your buying power given the rate of pay and cost of living in these cities.

You can work through a similar exercise for any type of job you are considering and for many locations when current salary information is available. It will be worth your time to undertake this analysis if you are seriously considering a relocation. By doing so you will be able to make an informed choice.

Step 4 Exploring Your Longer-Term Goals

There is no question that when we first begin working, our goals are to use our skills and education in a job that will reward us with employment, income, and status relative to the preparation we brought with us to this position. If we are not being paid as much as we feel we should for our level of education or if job demands don't provide the intellectual stimulation we had hoped for, we experience unhappiness and as a result often seek other employment.

Most jobs we consider "good" are those that fulfill our basic "lower-level" needs of security, food, clothing, shelter, income, and productive work. But even when our basic needs are met and our jobs are secure and productive, we as individuals are constantly changing. As we change, the demands and expectations we place on our jobs may change. Fortunately, some jobs grow and change with us, and this explains why some people are happy throughout many years in a job.

But more often people are bigger than the jobs they fill. We have more goals and needs than any job could satisfy. These are "higher-level" needs of self-esteem, companionship, affection, and an increasing desire to feel we are employing ourselves in the most effective way possible. Not all of these higher-level needs can be met through employment, but for as long as we are employed, we increasingly demand that our jobs play their part in moving us along the path to fulfillment.

Another obvious but important fact is that we change as we mature. Although our jobs also have the potential for change, they may not change as frequently or as markedly as we do. There are increasingly fewer one-job, one-employer careers; we must think about a work future that may involve voluntary or forced moves from employer to employer. Because of that very real possibility, we need to take advantage of the opportunities in each position we hold. Acquiring the skills and competencies associated with each position will keep us viable and attractive as employees. This is particularly true in a job market that not only is technology/computer dependent, but also is populated with more and more small, self-transforming organizations rather than the large, seemingly stable organizations of the past.

If you are considering a position as an art curator in a museum, you would gain a better perspective if you talked to an entry-level assistant registrar; a more experienced associate or full registrar; and, finally, a chief registrar, a director or department head who has a considerable work history in the field. Each will have a different perspective, unique concerns, and an individual set of values.

Step 5   Enumerating Your Skill Base

In terms of the job search, skills can be thought of as capabilities that can be developed in school, at work, or by volunteering and then used in specific job settings. Many studies have documented the kinds of skills that employers seek in entry-level applicants. For example, some of the most desired skills for individuals interested in the teaching profession are the ability to interact effectively with students one-on-one, to manage a classroom, to adapt to varying situations as necessary, and to get involved in school activities. Business employers have also identified important qualities, including enthusiasm for the employer's product or service, a businesslike mind, the ability to follow written or oral instructions, the ability to demonstrate self-control, the confidence to suggest new ideas, the ability to communicate with all members of a group, an awareness of cultural differences, and loyalty, to name just a few. You will find that many of these skills are also in the repertoire of qualities demanded in your college major.

To be successful in obtaining any given job, you must be able to demonstrate that you possess a certain mix of skills that will allow you to carry out the duties required by that job. This skill mix will vary a great deal from job to job; to determine the skills necessary for the jobs you are seeking, you can read job advertisements or more generic job descriptions, such as those found later in this book. If you want to be effective in the job search, you must directly show employers that you possess the skills needed to be successful in filling the position. These skills will initially be described on your résumé and then discussed again during the interview process.

Skills are either general or specific. To develop a list of skills relevant to employers, you must first identify the general skills you possess, then list specific skills you have to offer, and, finally, examine which of these skills employers are seeking.

Identifying Your General Skills. Because you possess or will possess a college degree, employers will assume that you can read and write, perform certain basic computations, think critically, and communicate effectively. Employers will want to see that you have acquired these skills, and they will want to know which additional general skills you possess.

One way to begin identifying skills is to write an experiential diary. An experiential diary lists all the tasks you were responsible for completing for each job you've held and then outlines the skills required to do those tasks. You may list several skills for any given task. This diary allows you to distinguish between the tasks you performed and the underlying skills required to complete those tasks. Here's an example:

For each job or experience you have participated in, develop a worksheet based on the example shown here. On a résumé, you may want to describe these skills rather than simply listing tasks. Skills are easier for the employer to appreciate, especially when your experience is very different from the

Tasks	Skills
Answering telephone	Effective use of language, clear diction, ability to direct inquiries, ability to solve problems
Waiting on tables	Poise under conditions of time and pressure, speed, accuracy, good memory, simultaneous completion of tasks, sales skills

employment you are seeking. In addition to helping you identify general skills, this experiential diary will prepare you to speak more effectively in an interview about the qualifications you possess.

Identifying Your Specific Skills. It may be easier to identify your specific skills because you can definitely say whether you can speak other languages, program a computer, draft a map or diagram, or edit a document using appropriate symbols and terminology.

Using your experiential diary, identify the points in your history where you learned how to do something very specific, and decide whether you have a beginning, intermediate, or advanced knowledge of how to use that particular skill. Right now, be sure to list *every* specific skill you have, and don't consider whether you like using the skill. Write down a list of specific skills you have acquired and the level of competence you possess—beginning, intermediate, or advanced.

Relating Your Skills to Employers. You probably have thought about a couple of different jobs you might be interested in obtaining, and one way to begin relating the general and specific skills you possess to a potential employer's needs is to read actual advertisements for these types of positions (see Part Two for resources listing actual job openings).

For example, you might be interested in a career as an art gallery manager. A typical job listing might read "Requires 2–5 years experience, organizational and interpersonal skills, imagination, drive, and the ability to work under pressure." If you then used any one of the general sources of information that describe the job of art gallery manager, you would find additional information. Art gallery managers also develop marketing plans, write and edit promotional material, work with staff and artists, and must be thoroughly knowledgeable about the art world.

Begin building a comprehensive list of required skills with the first job description you read. Exploring advertisements for and descriptions of several types of related positions will reveal a core of necessary skills. In building this list, include both general and specific skills.

The following is a sample list of skills needed to be successful as an art gallery manager. These items were extracted from general resources and actual job listings.

On a separate sheet of paper, try to generate a comprehensive list of required skills for at least one job you are considering.

JOB: ART GALLERY MANAGER

General Skills	Specific Skills
Disseminate information	Write public relations materials
Gather information	Select illustrations
Have a specific body of knowledge	Write letters
	Write memos
Work in a hectic environment	Have a professional phone presence
Present a certain image	Develop marketing plans
Work long hours near deadline	Arrange exhibits
	Display artwork
Work well with people	Schedule showings
Exhibit creativity	Write press releases
Exhibit drive	Have an eye for what will sell
Be able to work under pressure	Know the tastes of your customers
Be organized	
Be able to supervise the work of others	
Have excellent written and verbal skills	

The list of general skills that you develop for a given career path would be valuable for any number of jobs you might apply for. Many of the specific skills would also be transferable to other types of positions. For example, scheduling special exhibits would be a required skill for art gallery managers and for curators working in an art museum.

Now review the list of skills that are required for jobs you are considering, and check off those skills that *you know you possess*. You should refer to these specific skills on the résumé that you write for this type of job. See Chapter 2 for details on résumé writing.

Step 6   Recognizing Your Preferred Skills

In the previous section you developed a comprehensive list of skills that relate to particular career paths that are of interest to you. You can now relate these to skills that you prefer to use. We all use a wide range of skills (some researchers say individuals have a repertoire of about five hundred skills), but we may not particularly be interested in using all of them in our work. There may be some skills that come to us more naturally or that we use successfully time and time again and that we want to continue to use; these are best described as our preferred skills. For this exercise use the list of skills that you created for the previous section, and decide which of them you are *most interested in using* in future work and how often you would like to use them. You might be interested in using some skills only occasionally, while others you would like to use more regularly. You probably also have skills that you hope you can use constantly.

As you examine job announcements, look for matches between this list of preferred skills and the qualifications described in the advertisements. These skills should be highlighted on your résumé and discussed in job interviews.

Step 7   Assessing Skills Needing Further Development

Previously you compiled a list of general and specific skills required for given positions. You already possess some of these skills; those that remain to be developed are your underdeveloped skills.

If you are just beginning the job search, there may be gaps between the qualifications required for some of the jobs you're considering and the skills you possess. The thought of having to admit to and talk about these underdeveloped skills, especially in a job interview, is a frightening one. One way to put a healthy perspective on this subject is to target and relate your exploration of underdeveloped skills to the types of positions you are seeking. Recognizing these shortcomings and planning to overcome them with either on-the-job training or additional formal education can be a positive way to address the concept of underdeveloped skills.

On your worksheet or in your journal, make a list of up to five general or specific skills required for the positions you're interested in that you *don't currently possess*. For each item list an idea you have for specific action you could take to acquire that skill. Do some brainstorming to come up with possible actions. If you have a hard time generating ideas, talk to people currently working in this type of position, professionals in your college career services office, trusted friends, family members, or members of related professional associations.

In the chapter on interviewing, we will discuss in detail how to effectively address questions about underdeveloped skills. Generally speaking, though, employers want genuine answers to these types of questions. They want you to reveal "the real you," and they also want to see how you answer difficult questions. In taking the positive, targeted approach discussed above, you show the employer that you are willing to continue to learn and that you have a plan for strengthening your job qualifications.

Using Your Self-Assessment

Exploring entry-level career options can be an exciting experience if you have good resources available and will take the time to use them. Can you effectively complete the following tasks?

1. Understand your personality traits and relate them to career choices
2. Define your personal values
3. Determine your economic needs
4. Explore longer-term goals
5. Understand your skill base
6. Recognize your preferred skills
7. Express a willingness to improve on your underdeveloped skills

If so, then you can more meaningfully participate in the job search process by writing a more effective résumé, finding job titles that represent work you are interested in doing, locating job sites that will provide the opportunity for you to use your strengths and skills, networking in an informed way, participating in focused interviews, getting the most out of follow-up contacts, and evaluating job offers to find those that create a good match between you and the employer. The remaining chapters in Part One guide you through these next steps in the job search process. For many job seekers, this process can take anywhere from three months to a year to implement. The time you will need to put into your job search will depend on the type of job you want and the geographic location where you'd like to work. Think of your effort as a job in itself, requiring you to set aside time each week to complete the needed work. Carefully undertaken efforts may reduce the time you need for your job search.

2

The Résumé and Cover Letter

The task of writing a résumé may seem overwhelming if you are unfamiliar with this type of document, but there are some easily understood techniques that can and should be used. This section was written to help you understand the purpose of the résumé, the different types of résumé formats available, and how to write the sections of information traditionally found on a résumé. We will present examples and explanations that address questions frequently posed by people writing their first résumé or updating an old résumé.

Even within the formats and suggestions given, however, there are infinite variations. True, most résumés follow one of the outlines suggested, but you should feel free to adjust the résumé to suit your needs and make it expressive of your life and experience.

Why Write a Résumé?

The purpose of a résumé is to convince an employer that you should be interviewed. Whether you're mailing, faxing, or E-mailing this document, you'll want to present enough information to show that you can make an immediate and valuable contribution to an organization. A résumé is not an indepth historical or legal document; later in the job search process you may be asked to document your entire work history on an application form and attest to its validity. The résumé should, instead, highlight relevant information pertaining directly to the organization that will receive the document or to the type of position you are seeking.

We will discuss the chronological and digital résumés in detail here. Functional and targeted résumés, which are used much less often, are briefly discussed. The reasons for using one type of résumé over another and the typical format for each are addressed in the following sections.

The Chronological Résumé

The chronological résumé is the most common of the various résumé formats and therefore the format that employers are most used to receiving. This type of résumé is easy to read and understand because it details the chronological progression of jobs you have held. (See Exhibit 2.1.) It begins with your most recent employment and works back in time. If you have a solid work history or have experience that provided growth and development in your duties and responsibilities, a chronological résumé will highlight these achievements. The typical elements of a chronological résumé include the heading, a career objective, educational background, employment experience, activities, and references.

The Heading
The heading consists of your name, address, telephone number, and other means of contact. This may include a fax number, E-mail address, and your home-page address. If you are using a shared E-mail account or a parent's business fax, be sure to let others who use these systems know that you may receive important professional correspondence via these systems. You wouldn't want to miss a vital E-mail or fax! Likewise, if your résumé directs readers to a personal home page on the Web, be certain it's a professional personal home page designed to be viewed and appreciated by a prospective employer. This may mean making substantial changes in the home page you currently mount on the Web.

The Objective. Without a doubt the objective statement is the most challenging part of the résumé for most writers. Even for individuals who have decided on a career path, it can be difficult to encapsulate all they want to say in one or two brief sentences. For job seekers who are unfocused or unclear about their intentions, trying to write this section can inhibit the entire résumé writing process.

Keep the objective as short as possible and no longer than two short sentences.

Exhibit 2.1
CHRONOLOGICAL RÉSUMÉ

JULIE HAMPTON

Lantern Hall #324
Rhode Island School of Design
Providence, RI 03428
(401) 555-7500
(until May 2003)

3229 Greenwood Drive
Falls Church, VA 22432
(703) 555-8841

OBJECTIVE
A career in television graphic arts, initially as a graphic artist and ultimately as creative director.

EDUCATION
Bachelor of Arts in Commercial Art
Rhode Island School of Design, May 2003
Overall GPA 3.2 on a 4.0 scale

RELATED COURSES
Visual Communications in Television   Media and the Marketplace
Computer-Aided Design   Product Design

EXPERIENCE
Internship. ABC Studios, New York City, 2001 to present
Assistant to the Associate Creative Director on "All My Children" creating opening and closing credits and special effects.

Internship. WGBH—Public Television, Boston, academic year 2001–2002
Graphics department. Worked in a team environment, designed computer graphics for television programming, served as leader for award-winning documentary, "Opera in Boston."

Work-Study Program. *Washington Post*, summers 1998–2000
Advertising department. Produced layout for Sunday supplements, including photography and computer-aided design (CAD) for real estate section.

continued

PORTFOLIO
Color samples are attached. Complete portfolio is available.

REFERENCES
Both personal and professional references are available upon request.

Choose one of the following types of objective statement:

1. General Objective Statement

- An entry-level educational programming coordinator position

2. Position-Focused Objective

- To obtain the position of conference coordinator at State College

3. Industry-Focused Objective

- To begin a career as a sales representative in the cruise line industry

4. Summary of Qualifications Statement

> A degree in art history and four years of progressively increasing responsibilities in the curatorial department of a major museum have prepared me for a career as assistant curator in an institution that values hands-on involvement and thoroughness.

Support Your Objective. A résumé that contains any one of these types of objective statements should then go on to demonstrate why you are qualified to get the position. Listing academic degrees can be one way to indicate qualifications. Another demonstration would be in the way previous experiences, both volunteer and paid, are described. Without this kind of documentation in the body of the résumé, the objective looks unsupported. Think of the résumé as telling a connected story about you. All the elements should work together to form a coherent picture that ideally should relate to your statement of objective.

Education

This section of your résumé should indicate the exact name of the degree you will receive or have received, spelled out completely with no abbreviations. The degree is generally listed after the objective, followed by the institution name and location, and then the month and year of graduation. This section could also include your academic minor, grade point average (GPA), and appearance on the Dean's List or President's List.

If you have enough space, you might want to include a section listing courses related to the field in which you are seeking work. The best use of a "related courses" section would be to list some course work that is not traditionally associated with the major. Perhaps you took several computer courses outside your degree that will be helpful and related to the job prospects you are entertaining. Several education section examples are shown here:

- Bachelor of Arts degree in Arts Education, Elementary; Florida Atlantic University, Boca Raton, FL; December 2002. Minor: Child Development
- Bachelor of Arts degree in Art Education, Secondary; Tufts University, Medford, MA; May 2003
- Bachelor of Fine Arts Degree in Visual Arts, with a concentration in stained glass; Boston Museum School, Boston, MA; June 2003

An example of a format for related-courses section follows:

RELATED COURSES

Photography	Psychology
Public Speaking	Computer Graphics
Architectural Design	Research Methods

Experience

The experience section of your résumé should be the most substantial part and should take up most of the space on the page. Employers want to see what kind of work history you have. They will look at your range of experiences, longevity in jobs, and specific tasks you are able to complete. This section may also be called "work experience," "related experience," "employment history," or "employment." No matter what you call this section, some important points to remember are the following:

1. **Describe your duties** as they relate to the position you are seeking.
2. **Emphasize major responsibilities** and indicate increases in responsibility. Include all relevant employment experiences: summer, part-time, internships, cooperative education, or self-employment.
3. **Emphasize skills**, especially those that transfer from one situation to another. The fact that you coordinated a student organization, chaired meetings, supervised others, and managed a budget leads one to suspect that you could coordinate other things as well.
4. **Use descriptive job titles** that provide information about what you did. A "Student Intern" should be more specifically stated as, for example, "Magazine Operations Intern." "Volunteer" is also too general; a title such as "Peer Writing Tutor" would be more appropriate.
5. **Create word pictures** by using active verbs to start sentences. Describe *results* you have produced in the work you have done.

A limp description would say something such as the following: "My duties included helping with production, proofreading, and editing. I used a design and page layout program." An action statement would be stated as follows: "Coordinated and assisted in the creative marketing of brochures and seminar promotions, becoming proficient in Quark."

Remember, an accomplishment is simply a result, a final measurable product that people can relate to. A duty is not a result; it is an obligation—every job holder has duties. For an effective résumé, list as many results as you can. To make the most of the limited space you have and to give your description impact, carefully select appropriate and accurate descriptors.

Here are some traits that employers tell us they like to see:

- Teamwork
- Energy and motivation
- Learning and using new skills
- Versatility
- Critical thinking
- Understanding how profits are created
- Organizational acumen
- Communicating directly and clearly, in both writing and speaking

- Risk taking
- Willingness to admit mistakes
- High personal standards

Solutions to Frequently Encountered Problems

Repetitive Employment with the Same Employer
EMPLOYMENT: The Foot Locker, Portland, Oregon. Summer 2001, 2002, 2003. Initially employed in high school as salesclerk. Due to successful performance, asked to return next two summers at higher pay with added responsibility. Ranked as the #2 salesperson the first summer and #1 the next two summers. Assisted in arranging eye-catching retail displays; served as manager of other summer workers during owner's absence.

A Large Number of Jobs
EMPLOYMENT: Recent Hospitality Industry Experience: Affiliated with four upscale hotel/restaurant complexes (September 2001 February 2004), where I worked part- and full-time as a waiter, bartender, disc jockey, and bookkeeper to produce income for college.

Several Positions with the Same Employer
EMPLOYMENT: Coca-Cola Bottling Co., Burlington, Vermont, 2001–2004. In four years, I received three promotions, each with increased pay and responsibility.

Summer Sales Coordinator: Promoted to hire, train, and direct efforts of add-on staff of fifteen college-age route salespeople hired to meet summer peak demand for product.

Sales Administrator: Promoted to run home office sales desk, managing accounts and associated delivery schedules for professional sales force of ten people. Intensive phone work, daily interaction with all personnel, and strong knowledge of product line required.

Route Salesperson: Summer employment to travel and tourism industry sites that use Coke products. Met specific schedule demands, used good communication skills with wide variety of customers, and demonstrated strong selling skills. Named salesperson of the month for July and August of that year.

Questions Résumé Writers Often Ask

How Far Back Should I Go in Terms of Listing Past Jobs?

Usually, listing three or four jobs should suffice. If you did something back in high school that has a bearing on your future aspirations for employment, by all means list the job. As you progress through your college career, high school jobs will be replaced on the résumé by college employment.

Should I Differentiate Between Paid and Nonpaid Employment?

Most employers are not initially concerned about how much you were paid. They are anxious to know how much responsibility you held in your past employment. There is no need to specify that your work was as a volunteer if you had significant responsibilities.

How Should I Represent My Accomplishments or Work-Related Responsibilities?

Succinctly, but fully. In other words, give the employer enough information to arouse curiosity but not so much detail that you leave nothing to the imagination. Besides, some jobs merit more lengthy explanations than others. Be sure to convey any information that can give an employer a better understanding of the depth of your involvement at work. Did you supervise others? How many? Did your efforts result in a more efficient operation? How much did you increase efficiency? Did you handle a budget? How much? Were you promoted in a short time? Did you work two jobs at once or fifteen hours per week after high school? Where appropriate, quantify.

Should the Work Section Always Follow the Education Section on the Résumé?

Always lead with your strengths. If your education closely relates to the employment you now seek, put this section after the objective. If your education does not closely relate but you have a surplus of good work experiences, consider reversing the order of your sections to lead with employment, followed by education.

How Should I Present My Activities, Honors, Awards, Professional Societies, and Affiliations?

This section of the résumé can add valuable information for an employer to consider if used correctly. The rule of thumb for information in this section is to include only those activities that are in some way relevant to the objective stated on your résumé. If you can draw a valid connection between your activities and your objective, include them; if not, leave them out.

Professional affiliations and honors should all be listed; especially important are those related to your job objective. Social clubs and activities need not be a part of your résumé unless you hold a significant office or you are looking for a position related to your membership. Be aware that most prospective employers' principal concerns are related to your employability, not your social life. If you have any, publications can be included as an addendum to your résumé.

How Should I Handle References?

The use of references is considered a part of the interview process, and they should never be listed on a résumé. You would always provide references to a potential employer if requested to, so it is not even necessary to include this section on the résumé if space does not permit. If space is available, it is acceptable to include the following statement:

- REFERENCES: Furnished upon request.

The Functional Résumé

The functional résumé departs from a chronological résumé in that it organizes information by specific accomplishments in various settings: previous jobs, volunteer work, associations, and so forth. This type of résumé permits you to stress the substance of your experiences rather than the position titles you have held. You should consider using a functional résumé if you have held a series of similar jobs that relied on the same skills or abilities. There are many good books in which you can find examples of functional résumés, including *How to Write a Winning Resume* or *Resumes Made Easy*.

The Targeted Résumé

The targeted résumé focuses on specific work-related capabilities you can bring to a given position within an organization. Past achievements are listed to highlight your capabilities and the work history section is abbreviated.

Exhibit 2.2
DIGITAL RÉSUMÉ

CYNTHIA PORTER   ◄——————————— Put your name at the
333 W. Belmont Ave.   top on its own line.
Chicago, IL 60657
Phone: 773/555-8430   ◄——————————— Put your phone number
E-mail: cyporter@xxx.com   on its own line.

KEYWORD SUMMARY   ◄——————————— Keywords make your
BFA Advertising Design   résumé easier to find in
Art Director   a database.
QuarkXPress, Adobe Photoshop,
    Adobe Illustrator, Paache Airbrush   Use a standard-width
                                                                          typeface.

WORK EXPERIENCE
Media Features Syndicate, Chicago
Art Director/Print Production Manager
1995-Present
* Supervise 20 employees in the layout and printing ◄—— Use a space between
of syndicated newspaper articles, comics, and   asterisk and text.
puzzles for national newspapers.
* Manage electronic pre-press section and schedule
promotional ads.   No line should exceed
* Design and quality-check covers for newspaper   sixty-five characters.
TV guides.

Harrington Studios, New York   End each line by
Freelance Graphic Artist   hitting the ENTER (or
1991-1995   RETURN) key.
* Designed promotional and direct mail materials for
clients in the performing arts and fashion industries.
* Developed concepts for press kits and corporate
identities.

EDUCATION ◄———————————————— Capitalize letters to
BFA Advertising Design, 1994   emphasize headings.
Syracuse University, NY

Digital Résumés

Today's employers have to manage an enormous number of résumés. One of the most frequent complaints the writers of this series hear from students is the failure of employers to even acknowledge the receipt of a résumé and cover letter. Frequently, the reason for this poor response or nonresponse is the volume of applications received for every job. In an attempt to better manage the considerable labor investment involved in processing large numbers of résumés, many employers are requiring digital submission of résumés. There are two types of digital résumés: those that can be E-mailed or posted to a website, called *electronic résumés*, and those that can be "read" by a computer, commonly called *scannable résumés*. Though the format may be a bit different from the traditional "paper" résumé, the goal of both types of digital résumés is the same—to get you an interview! These résumés must be designed to be "technologically friendly." What that basically means to you is that they should be free of graphics and fancy formatting. (See Exhibit 2.2.)

Electronic Résumés

Sometimes referred to as plain-text résumés, electronic résumés are designed to be E-mailed to an employer or posted to one of many commercial Internet databases such as CareerMosaic.com, America's Job Bank (ajb.dni.us), or Monster.com.

Some technical considerations:

- Electronic résumés must be written in American Standard Code for Information Interchange (ASCII), which is simply a plain-text format. These characters are universally recognized so that every computer can accurately read and understand them. To create an ASCII file of your current résumé, open your document, then save it as a text or ASCII file. This will eliminate all formatting. Edit as needed using your computer's text editor application.
- Use a standard-width typeface. Courier is a good choice because it is the font associated with ASCII in most systems.
- Use a font size of 11 to 14 points. A 12-point font is considered standard.
- Your margin should be left-justified.
- Do not exceed sixty-five characters per line because the word-wrap function doesn't operate in ASCII.

- Do not use boldface, italics, underlining, bullets, or various font sizes. Instead, use asterisks, plus signs, or all capital letters when you want to emphasize something.
- Avoid graphics and shading.
- Use as many "keywords" as you possibly can. These are words or phrases usually relating to skills or experience that either are specifically used in the job announcement or are popular buzzwords in the industry.
- Minimize abbreviations.
- Your name should be the first line of text.
- Conduct a "test run" by E-mailing your résumé to yourself and a friend before you send it to the employer. See how it transmits, and make any changes you need to. Continue to test it until it's exactly how you want it to look.
- Unless an employer specifically requests that you send the résumé in the form of an attachment, don't. Employers can encounter problems opening a document as an attachment, and there are always viruses to consider.
- Don't forget your cover letter. Send it along with your résumé as a single message.

Scannable Résumés

Some companies are relying on technology to narrow the candidate pool for available job openings. Electronic Applicant Tracking uses imaging to scan, sort, and store résumé elements in a database. Then, through OCR (Optical Character Recognition) software, the computer scans the résumés for keywords and phrases. To have the best chance at getting an interview, you want to increase the number of "hits"—matches of your skills, abilities, experience, and education to those the computer is scanning for—your résumé will get. You can see how critical using the right keywords is for this type of résumé.

Technical considerations include:

- Again, do not use boldface (newer systems may read this OK, but many older ones won't), italics, underlining, bullets, shading, graphics, or multiple font sizes. Instead, for emphasis, use asterisks, plus signs, or all capital letters. Minimize abbreviations.
- Use a popular typeface such as Courier, Helvetica, Ariel, or Palatino. Avoid decorative fonts.
- Font size should be between 11 and 14 points.

- Do not compress the spacing between letters.
- Use horizontal and vertical lines sparingly; the computer may misread them as the letters L or I.
- Left-justify the text.
- Do not use parentheses or brackets around telephone numbers, and be sure your phone number is on its own line of text.
- Your name should be the first line of text and on its own line. If your résumé is longer than one page, be sure to put your name on the top of all pages.
- Use a traditional résumé structure. The chronological format may work best.
- Use nouns that are skill-focused, such as *management, writer,* and *programming.* This is different from traditional paper résumés, which use action-oriented verbs.
- Laser printers produce the finest copies. Avoid dot-matrix printers.
- Use standard, light-colored paper with text on one side only. Since the higher the contrast, the better, your best choice is black ink on white paper.
- Always send original copies. If you must fax, set the fax on fine mode, not standard.
- Do not staple or fold your résumé. This can confuse the computer.
- Before you send your scannable résumé, be certain the employer uses this technology. If you can't determine this, you may want to send two versions (scannable and traditional) to be sure your résumé gets considered.

Résumé Production and Other Tips

An ink-jet printer is the preferred option for printing your résumé. Begin by printing just a few copies. You may find a small error or you may simply want to make some changes, and it is less frustrating and less expensive if you print in small batches.

Résumé paper color should be carefully chosen. You should consider the types of employers who will receive your résumé and the types of positions for which you are applying. Use white or ivory paper for traditional or conservative employers or for higher-level positions.

Black ink on sharp, white paper can be harsh on the reader's eyes. Think about an ivory or cream paper that will provide less contrast and be easier to read. Pink, green, and blue tints should generally be avoided.

Many résumé writers buy packages of matching envelopes and cover sheet stationery that, although not absolutely necessary, help convey a professional impression.

If you'll be producing many cover letters at home, be sure you have high-quality printing equipment. Learn standard envelope formats for business, and retain a copy of every cover letter you send out. You can use the copies to take notes of any telephone conversations that may occur.

If attending a job fair, either carry a briefcase or place your résumé in a nicely covered legal-size pad holder.

The Cover Letter

The cover letter provides you with the opportunity to tailor your résumé by telling the prospective employer how you can be a benefit to the organization. It allows you to highlight aspects of your background that are not already discussed in your résumé and that might be especially relevant to the organization you are contacting or to the position you are seeking. Every résumé should have a cover letter enclosed when you send it out. Unlike the résumé, which may be mass-produced, a cover letter is most effective when it is individually prepared and focused on the particular requirements of the organization in question.

A good cover letter should supplement the résumé and motivate the reader to review the résumé. The format shown in Exhibit 2.3 is only a suggestion to help you decide what information to include in writing a cover letter.

Begin the cover letter with your street address six lines down from the top. Leave three to five lines between the date and the name of the person to whom you are addressing the cover letter. Make sure you leave one blank line between the salutation and the body of the letter and between paragraphs. After typing "Sincerely," leave four blank lines and type your name. This should leave plenty of room for your signature. A sample cover letter is shown in Exhibit 2.4.

The following guidelines will help you write good cover letters:

1. Be sure to type your letter neatly; ensure there are no misspellings.
2. Avoid unusual typefaces, such as script.
3. Address the letter to an individual, using the person's name and title. To obtain this information, call the company. If answering a blind newspaper advertisement, address the letter "To Whom It May Concern" or omit the salutation.

Exhibit 2.3
COVER LETTER FORMAT

Your Street Address
Your Town, State, Zip
Phone Number
Fax Number
E-mail

Date

Name
Title
Organization
Address

Dear _____ :

First Paragraph. In this paragraph state the reason for the letter, name the specific position or type of work you are applying for, and indicate from which resource (career services office, website, newspaper, contact, employment service) you learned of this opening. The first paragraph can also be used to inquire about future openings.

Second Paragraph. Indicate why you are interested in this position, the company, or its products or services, and what you can do for the employer. If you are a recent graduate, explain how your academic background makes you a qualified candidate. Try not to repeat the same information found in the résumé.

Third Paragraph. Refer the reader to the enclosed résumé for more detailed information.

Fourth Paragraph. In this paragraph say what you will do to follow up on your letter. For example, state that you will call by a certain date to set up an interview or to find out if the company will be recruiting in your area. Finish by indicating your willingness to answer any questions the recipient may have. Be sure you have provided your phone number.

Sincerely,

Type your name
Enclosure

Exhibit 2.4
SAMPLE COVER LETTER

146 Brainard Road #24
Brighton, MA 02135
(617) 555-3333

May 10, 2003

Diana Jackson
Director of Personnel
Sterling Museum
65 The Fenway
Boston, MA 02115

Dear Ms. Jackson:

In June of 2003 I will graduate from Northeastern University with a bachelor of arts degree in museum studies. I read of your opening for an assistant collections manager in *The Globe*, and I am very interested in the possibilities it offers. I am writing to explore the opportunity for employment with your museum.

The ad indicated that you were looking for creative team players with good communication skills and art collection management experience. I believe that I possess those qualities. Through my placement at the Boston Museum of Fine Arts with Northeastern's cooperative education program, I learned the ins and outs of the workings of a major museum, including the importance of teamwork.

In addition to the various museums studies courses in my academic program, I felt it important to enroll in some art and computer courses such as art history and the use of spreadsheets and databases. These courses helped me become familiar with the wide range of museum collections, while at the same time familiarizing myself with a variety of computer tracking systems. I believe that, coupled with my enthusiasm for working in an art museum environment, these traits will help me represent Sterling Museum in a professional and enthusiastic manner.

As you will see by my enclosed résumé, I worked at the Museum of Fine Arts for a total of three years, in both the registrar's office and under the direction of the curator of eighteenth-century European art. These placements provided me with experience handling and exhibiting artwork and allowed me to see how both offices function cooperatively.

I would like to meet with you to discuss how my education and experience would be consistent with your needs. I will contact your office next week to discuss the possibility of an interview. In the meantime, if you have any questions or require additional information, please contact me at my home, (617) 555-4536.

Sincerely,

Jill Browne
Enclosure

4. Be sure your cover letter directly indicates the position you are applying for and tells why you are qualified to fill it.
5. Send the original letter, not a photocopy, with your résumé. Keep a copy for your records.
6. Make your cover letter no more than one page.
7. Include a phone number where you can be reached.
8. Avoid trite language and have someone read the letter over to react to its tone, content, and mechanics.
9. For your own information, record the date you send out each letter and résumé.

3

Researching Careers and Networking

One common question a career counselor encounters is "What can I do with my degree?" Art majors have narrowed their interests a little more successfully than other liberal arts graduates, but still, all the choices are not defined clearly. Art history majors or B.F.A. graduates can often struggle with this problem because unlike their fellow students in more applied fields, such as accounting, computer science, or health and physical education, there is real confusion about just what kinds of jobs, other than the obvious route of teaching or museum work, they can do with their degree. Accounting majors become accountants, computer science majors can work as data analysts. What specific jobs are open to art majors?

What Do They Call the Job You Want?

One reason for confusion is perhaps a mistaken assumption that a college education provides job training. In most cases it does not. Of course, applied fields such as engineering, management, or education provide specific skills for the workplace as well as an education. Regardless, your overall college education exposes you to numerous fields of study and teaches you quantitative reasoning, critical thinking, writing, and speaking, all of which can be successfully applied to a number of different job fields. But it still remains up to you to choose a job field and to learn how to articulate the benefits of your education in a way the employer will appreciate.

Collecting Job Titles

The world of employment is a complex place, so you need to become a bit of an explorer and adventurer and be willing to try a variety of techniques to develop a list of possible occupations that might use your talents and education. You might find computerized interest inventories, reference books and other sources, and classified ads helpful in this respect. Once you have a list of possibilities that you are interested in and qualified for, you can move on to find out what kinds of organizations have these job titles.

Computerized Interest Inventories. One way to begin collecting job titles is to identify a number of jobs that call for your degree and the particular skills and interests you identified as part of the self-assessment process. There are excellent interactive career-guidance programs on the market to help you produce such selected lists of possible job titles. Most of these are available at colleges and at some larger town and city libraries. Two of the industry leaders are *CHOICES* and *DISCOVER*. Both allow you to enter interests, values, educational background, and other information to produce lists of possible occupations and industries. Each of the resources listed here will produce different job title lists. Some job titles will appear again and again, while others will be unique to a particular source. Investigate all of them!

Reference Sources. Books on the market that may be available through your local library or career counseling office also suggest various occupations related to specific majors. The following are only a few of the many good books on the market: *The College Board Guide to 150 Popular College Majors, College Majors and Careers: A Resource Guide for Effective Life Planning* both by Paul Phifer, and *Kaplan's What to Study: 101 Fields in a Flash*. All of these books list possible job titles within the academic major.

There are dozens of possible job titles for those interested in pursuing a career in art. Some are familiar ones, such as artist or teacher, and others are interestingly different, such as art critic or interior designer.

The *Occupational Thesaurus* is a good resource for researching job titles because it lists possibilities under general categories. Under "advertising," for example, you'll find a list of more than twenty associated job titles including manufacturer's representative and customer relations specialist. So if advertising was a suggested job title for you, this source adds some depth by suggesting a number of different occupations within that field.

Each job title deserves your consideration. Like removing the layers of an onion, the search for job titles can go on and on! As you spend time doing this activity, you are actually learning more about the value of your degree. What's important in your search at this point is not to become critical or selective but rather to develop as long a list of possibilities as you can. Every source used will help you add new and potentially exciting jobs to your growing list.

Classified Ads. It has been well publicized that the classified ad section of the newspaper represents only a small fraction of the current job market. Nevertheless, the weekly classified ads can be a great help to you in your search. Although they may not be the best place to look for a job, they can teach you a lot about the job market. Classified ads provide a good education in job descriptions, duties, responsibilities, and qualifications. In addition, they provide insight into which industries are actively recruiting and some indication of the area's employment market. This is particularly helpful when seeking a position in a specific geographic area and/or a specific field. For your purposes, classified ads are a good source for job titles to add to your list.

Read the Sunday classified ads in a major market newspaper for several weeks in a row. Cut and paste all the ads that interest you and seem to call for something close to your education, skills, experience, and interests. Remember that classified ads are written for what an organization *hopes* to find, you don't have to meet absolutely every criterion. However, if certain requirements are stated as absolute minimums and you cannot meet them, it's best not to waste your time and that of the employer.

The weekly classified want ads exercise is important because these jobs are out in the marketplace. They truly exist, and people with your qualifications are being sought to apply. What's more, many of these advertisements describe the duties and responsibilities of the job advertised and give you a beginning sense of the challenges and opportunities such a position presents. Some will indicate salary, and that will be helpful as well. This information will better define the jobs for you and provide some good material for possible interviews in that field.

Exploring Job Descriptions

Once you've arrived at a solid list of possible job titles that interest you and for which you believe you are somewhat qualified, it's a good idea to do some research on each of these jobs. The preeminent source for such job information is the *Dictionary of Occupational Titles*, or *DOT* (wave.net/upg/immigration/dot_index.html). This directory lists every conceivable job and provides excellent up-to-date information on duties and responsibilities, interactions with associates, and day-to-day assignments and tasks. These descriptions provide a thorough job analysis, but they do not consider the possible employers or the environments in which a job may be performed. So, although a position as public relations officer may be well defined in terms of duties and responsibilities, it does not explain the differences in doing public relations work in a college or a hospital or a factory or a bank. You will need to look somewhere else for work settings.

Learning More About Possible Work Settings

After reading some job descriptions, you may choose to edit and revise your list of job titles once again, discarding those you feel are not suitable and keeping those that continue to hold your interest. Or you may wish to keep your list intact and see where these jobs may be located. For example, if you are interested in public relations and you appear to have those skills and the requisite education, you'll want to know what organizations do public relations. How can you find that out? How much income does someone in public relations make a year and what is the employment potential for the field of public relations?

To answer these and many other questions about your list of job titles, we recommend you try any of the following resources: *Careers Encyclopedia*, the professional societies and resources found throughout this book, *College to Career: The Guide to Job Opportunities*, and the *Occupational Outlook Handbook* (http://stats.bls.gov/ocohome.htm). Each of these resources, in a different way, will help to put the job titles you have selected into an employer context. Perhaps the most extensive discussion is found in the *Occupational Outlook Handbook*, which gives a thorough presentation of the nature of the work, the working conditions, employment statistics, training, other qualifications, and advancement possibilities as well as job outlook and earnings. Related occupations are also detailed, and a select bibliography is provided to help you find additional information.

Continuing with our public relations example, your search through these reference materials would teach you that the public relations jobs you find attractive are available in larger hospitals, financial institutions, most corporations (both consumer goods and industrial goods), media organizations, and colleges and universities.

Networking

Networking is the process of deliberately establishing relationships to get career-related information or to alert potential employers that you are available for work. Networking is critically important to today's job seeker for two reasons: it will help you get the information you need, and it can help you find out about *all* of the available jobs.

Getting the Information You Need

Networkers will review your résumé and give you feedback on its effectiveness. They will talk about the job you are looking for and give you a candid appraisal of how they see your strengths and weaknesses. If they have a good sense of the industry or the employment sector for that job, you'll get their feelings on future trends in the industry as well. Some networkers will be very forthcoming about salaries, job-hunting techniques, and suggestions for your job search strategy. Many have been known to place calls right from the interview desk to friends and associates who might be interested in you. Each networker will make his or her own contribution, and each will be valuable.

Because organizations must evolve to adapt to current global market needs, the information provided by decision makers within various organizations will be critical to your success as a new job market entrant. For example, you might learn about the concept of virtual organizations from a networker. Virtual organizations coordinate economic activity to deliver value to customers by using resources outside the traditional boundaries of the organization. This concept is being discussed and implemented by chief executive officers of many organizations, including Ford Motor, Dell, and IBM. Networking can help you find out about this and other trends currently affecting the industries under your consideration.

Finding Out About All of the Available Jobs

Not every job that is available at this very moment is advertised for potential applicants to see. This is called the *hidden job market*. Only 15 to 20 percent of all jobs are formally advertised, which means that 80 to 85 percent of available jobs do not appear in published channels. Networking will help you become more knowledgeable about all the employment opportunities available during your job search period.

Although someone you might talk to today doesn't know of any openings within his or her organization, tomorrow or next week or next month an opening may occur. If you've taken the time to show an interest in and knowledge of their organization, if you've shown the company representative how you can help achieve organizational goals and that you can fit into the organization, you'll be one of the first candidates considered for the position.

Networking: A Proactive Approach

Networking is a proactive rather than a reactive approach. You, as a job seeker, are expected to initiate a certain level of activity on your own behalf; you cannot afford to simply respond to jobs listed in the newspaper. Being proactive means building a network of contacts that includes informed and interested decision makers who will provide you with up-to-date knowledge of the current job market and increase your chances of finding out about employment opportunities appropriate for your interests, experience, and level of education. An old axiom of networking says, "You are only two phone calls away from the information you need." In other words, by talking to enough people, you will quickly come across someone who can offer you help.

Preparing to Network

In deliberately establishing relationships, maximize your efforts by organizing your approach. Five specific areas in which you can organize your efforts include reviewing your self-assessment, reviewing your research on job sites and organizations, deciding who it is you want to talk to, keeping track of all your efforts, and creating your self-promotion tools.

Review Your Self-Assessment

Your self-assessment is as important a tool in preparing to network as it has been in other aspects of your job search. You have carefully evaluated your personal traits, personal values, economic needs, longer-term goals, skill base, preferred skills, and underdeveloped skills. During the networking process you will be called upon to communicate what you know about yourself and relate it to the information or job you seek. Be sure to review the exercises that you completed in the self-assessment section of this book in preparation for networking. We've explained that you need to assess what skills you have acquired from your major that are of general value to an employer and to be ready to express those in ways employers can appreciate as useful in their own organizations.

Review Research on Job Sites and Organizations

In addition, individuals assisting you will expect that you'll have at least some background information on the occupation or industry of interest to you. Refer to the appropriate sections of this book and other relevant publications to acquire the background information necessary for effective networking. They'll explain how to identify not only the job titles that might be of interest to you but also what kinds of organizations employ people to do that job. You will develop some sense of working conditions and expectations about duties and responsibilities—all of which will be of help in your networking interviews.

Decide Who It Is You Want to Talk To

Networking cannot begin until you decide who it is that you want to talk to and, in general, what type of information you hope to gain from your contacts. Once you know this, it's time to begin developing a list of contacts. Five useful sources for locating contacts are described here.

College Alumni Network. Most colleges and universities have created a formal network of alumni and friends of the institution who are particularly interested in helping currently enrolled students and graduates of their alma mater gain employment-related information.

It is usually a simple process to make use of an alumni network. Visit your college's website and locate the alumni office and/or your career center. Either or both sites will have information about your school's alumni network. You'll be provided with information on shadowing experiences, geographic information, or those alumni offering job referrals. If you don't find what you're looking for, don't hesitate to phone or E-mail your career center and ask what they can do to help you connect with an alum.

Alumni networkers may provide some combination of the following services: day-long shadowing experiences, telephone interviews, in-person interviews, information on relocating to given geographic areas, internship information, suggestions on graduate school study, and job vacancy notices.

Present and Former Supervisors. If you believe you are on good terms with present or former job supervisors, they may be an excellent resource for providing information or directing you to appropriate resources that would have information related to your current interests and needs. Additionally, these supervisors probably belong to professional organizations that they might be willing to utilize to get information for you.

Employers in Your Area. Although you may be interested in working in a geographic location different from the one where you currently reside, don't overlook the value of the knowledge and contacts those around you are able to provide. Use the local telephone directory and newspaper to identify the types of organizations you are thinking of working for or professionals who have the kinds of jobs you are interested in. Recently, a call made to a local hospital's financial administrator for information on working in health-care financial administration yielded more pertinent information on training seminars, regional professional organizations, and potential employment sites than a national organization was willing to provide.

Employers in Geographic Areas Where You Hope to Work. If you are thinking about relocating, identifying prospective employers or informational contacts in the new location will be critical to your success. Here are some tips for online searching. First, use a "metasearch" engine to get the most out of your search. Metasearch engines combine several engines into one powerful tool. We frequently use dogpile.com and metasearch.com for this purpose. Try using the city and state as your keywords in a search. *New Haven, Connecticut* will bring you to the city's website with links to the chamber of commerce, member businesses, and other valuable resources. By using looksmart.com you can locate newspapers in any area, and they, too, can provide valuable insight before you relocate. Of course, both dogpile and metasearch can lead you to yellow and white page directories in areas you are considering.

Professional Associations and Organizations. Professional associations and organizations can provide valuable information in several areas: career paths that you might not have considered, qualifications relating to those career choices, publications that list current job openings, and workshops or seminars that will enhance your professional knowledge and skills. They can also be excellent sources for background information on given industries: their health, current problems, and future challenges.

There are several excellent resources available to help you locate professional associations and organizations that would have information to meet your needs. Two especially useful publications are the *Encyclopedia of Associations* and *National Trade and Professional Associations of the United States.*

Keep Track of All Your Efforts

It can be difficult, almost impossible, to remember all the details related to each contact you make during the networking process, so you will want to develop a record-keeping system that works for you. Formalize this process by using your computer to keep a record of the people and organizations you want to contact. You can simply record the contact's name, address, and telephone number, and what information you hope to gain.

You could record this as a simple Word document and you could still use the "Find" function if you were trying to locate some data and could only recall the firm's name or the contact's name. If you're comfortable with database management and you have some database software on your computer, then you can put information at your fingertips even if you have only the zip code! The point here is not technological sophistication but good record keeping.

Once you have created this initial list, it will be helpful to keep more detailed information as you begin to actually make the contacts. Those details should include complete contact information, the date and content of each contact, names and information for additional networkers, and required follow-up. Don't forget to send a letter thanking your contact for his or her time! Your contact will appreciate your recall of details of your meetings and conversations, and the information will help you to focus your networking efforts.

Create Your Self-Promotion Tools

There are two types of promotional tools that are used in the networking process. The first is a résumé and cover letter, and the second is a one-minute "infomercial," which may be given over the telephone or in person.

Techniques for writing an effective résumé and cover letter are discussed in Chapter 2. Once you have reviewed that material and prepared these important documents, you will have created one of your self-promotion tools.

The one-minute infomercial will demand that you begin tying your interests, abilities, and skills to the people or organizations you want to network with. Think about your goal for making the contact to help you understand what you should say about yourself. You should be able to express yourself easily and convincingly. If, for example, you are contacting an alumnus of your institution to obtain the names of possible employment sites in a distant city, be prepared to discuss why you are interested in moving to that location, the types of jobs you are interested in, and the skills and abilities you possess that will make you a qualified candidate.

To create a meaningful one-minute infomercial, write it out, practice it as if it will be a spoken presentation, rewrite it, and practice it again if necessary until expressing yourself comes easily and is convincing.

Here's a simplified example of an infomercial for use over the telephone:

Hello, Ms. Regan? My name is Jacqueline Conlon. I am a recent graduate of Assumption College, and I want to enter the publishing field as a book jacket designer. I was an art major and feel confident that I have many of the skills that are valued in this line of work. I have strong design skills, including familiarity with desktop publishing software.

Ms. Regan, I'm calling you because I still need more information about entering the publishing field with an art degree. I'm hoping you have the time to sit down with me for about half an hour and discuss how attractive my résumé might be to a publishing house. I certainly am not averse to additional education, but I'm eager to begin work and I hope to acquire some good on-the-job training.

Would you be willing to talk with me? I would greatly appreciate it. I'm available most mornings, if that's convenient for you.

It very well may happen that your employer contact wishes you to communicate by E-mail. The infomercial quoted above could easily be rewritten for an E-mail message. You should "cut and paste" your résumé right into the E-mail text itself.

Other effective self-promotion tools include portfolios for those in the arts, writing professions, or teaching. Portfolios show examples of work, photographs of projects or classroom activities, or certificates and credentials that are job related. There may not be an opportunity to use the portfolio during an interview, and it is not something that should be left with the organization. It is designed to be explained and displayed by the creator. However, during some networking meetings, there may be an opportunity to illustrate a point or strengthen a qualification by exhibiting the portfolio.

Beginning the Networking Process

Set the Tone for Your Communications

It can be useful to establish "tone words" for any communications you embark upon. Before making your first telephone call or writing your first letter, decide what you want the person to think of you. If you are networking to try to obtain a job, your tone words might include descriptors such as *genuine*, *informed*, and *self-knowledgeable*. When you're trying to acquire information, your tone words may have a slightly different focus, such as *courteous*, *organized*, *focused*, and *well-spoken*. Use the tone words you establish for your contacts to guide you through the networking process.

Honestly Express Your Intentions

When contacting individuals, it is important to be honest about your reasons for making the contact. Establish your purpose in your own mind and be able and ready to articulate it concisely. Determine an initial agenda, whether it be informational questioning or self-promotion, present it to your contact, and be ready to respond immediately. If you don't adequately prepare before initiating your overture, you may find yourself at a disadvantage if you're asked to immediately begin your informational interview or self-promotion during the first phone conversation or visit.

Start Networking Within Your Circle of Confidence

Once you have organized your approach—by utilizing specific researching methods, creating a system for keeping track of the people you will contact, and developing effective self-promotion tools—you are ready to begin networking. The best way to begin networking is by talking with a group of people you trust and feel comfortable with. This group is usually made up of your family, friends, and career counselors. No matter who is in this inner circle, they will have a special interest in seeing you succeed in your job search. In addition, because they will be easy to talk to, you should try taking some risks in terms of practicing your information-seeking approach. Gain confidence in talking about the strengths you bring to an organization and the underdeveloped skills you feel hinder your candidacy. Be sure to review the section on self-assessment for tips on approaching each of these areas. Ask for critical but constructive feedback from the people in your circle of confidence on the letters you write and the one-minute infomercial you have developed. Evaluate whether you want to make the changes they suggest, then practice the changes on others within this circle.

Stretch the Boundaries of Your Networking Circle of Confidence

Once you have refined the promotional tools you will use to accomplish your networking goals, you will want to make additional contacts. Because you will not know most of these people, it will be a less comfortable activity to undertake. The practice that you gained with your inner circle of trusted friends should have prepared you to now move outside of that comfort zone.

It is said that any information a person needs is only two phone calls away, but the information cannot be gained until you (1) make a reasonable guess about who might have the information you need and (2) pick up the telephone to make the call. Using your network list that includes alumni, instructors, supervisors, employers, and associations, you can begin preparing your list of questions that will allow you to get the information you need.

Prepare the Questions You Want to Ask

Networkers can provide you with the insider's perspective on any given field and you can ask them questions that you might not want to ask in an interview. For example, you can ask them to describe the more repetitious or mundane parts of the job or ask them for a realistic idea of salary expectations. Be sure to prepare your questions ahead of time so that you are organized and efficient.

Be Prepared to Answer Some Questions

To communicate effectively, you must anticipate questions that will be asked of you by the networkers you contact. Revisit the self-assessment process you undertook and the research you've done so that you can effortlessly respond to questions about your short- and long-term goals and the kinds of jobs you are most interested in pursuing.

General Networking Tips

Make Every Contact Count. Setting the tone for each interaction is critical. Approaches that will help you communicate in an effective way include politeness, being appreciative of time provided to you, and being prepared and thorough. Remember, *everyone* within an organization has a circle of influence, so be prepared to interact effectively with each person you encounter in the networking process, including secretarial and support staff. Many information or job seekers have thwarted their own efforts by being rude to some individuals they encountered as they networked because they made the incorrect assumption that certain persons were unimportant.

Sometimes your contacts may be surprised at their ability to help you. After meeting and talking with you, they might think they have not offered much in the way of help. A day or two later, however, they may make a contact that would be useful to you and refer you to that person.

With Each Contact, Widen Your Circle of Networkers. Always leave an informational interview with the names of at least two more people who can help you get the information or job that you are seeking. Don't be shy about asking for additional contacts; networking is all about increasing the number of people you can interact with to achieve your goals.

Make Your Own Decisions. As you talk with different people and get answers to the questions you pose, you may hear conflicting information or get conflicting suggestions. Your job is to listen to these "experts" and decide what information and which suggestions will help you achieve *your* goals. Only implement those suggestions that you believe will work for you.

Shutting Down Your Network

As you achieve the goals that motivated your networking activity—getting the information you need or the job you want—the time will come to inactivate all or parts of your network. As you do, be sure to tell your primary supporters about your change in status. Call or write to each one of them and give them as many details about your new status as you feel is necessary to maintain a positive relationship.

Because a network takes on a life of its own, activity undertaken on your behalf will continue even after you cease your efforts. As you get calls or are contacted in some fashion, be sure to inform these networkers about your change in status, and thank them for assistance they have provided.

Information on the latest employment trends indicates that workers will change jobs or careers several times in their lifetime. Networking, then, will be a critical aspect in the span of your professional life. If you carefully and thoughtfully conduct your networking activities during your job search, you will have a solid foundation of experience when you need to network the next time around.

Where Are These Jobs, Anyway?

Having a list of job titles that you've designed around your own career interests and skills is an excellent beginning. It means you've really thought about who you are and what you are presenting to the employment market.

It has caused you to think seriously about the most appealing environments to work in, and you have identified some employer types that represent these environments.

The research and the thinking that you've done thus far will be used again and again. They will be helpful in writing your résumé and cover letters, in talking about yourself on the telephone to prospective employers, and in answering interview questions.

Now is a good time to begin to narrow the field of job titles and employment sites down to some specific employers to initiate the employment contact.

Finding Out Which Employers Hire People Like You

This section will provide tips, techniques, and specific resources for developing an actual list of specific employers that can be used to make contacts. It is only an outline that you must be prepared to tailor to your own particular needs and according to what you bring to the job search. Once again, it is important to communicate with others along the way exactly what you're looking for and what your goals are for the research you're doing. Librarians, employers, career counselors, friends, friends of friends, business contacts, and bookstore staff will all have helpful information on geographically specific and new resources to aid you in locating employers who'll hire you.

Identifying Information Resources

Your interview wardrobe and your new résumé might have put a dent in your wallet, but the resources you'll need to pursue your job search are available for free. The categories of information detailed here are not hard to find and are yours for the browsing.

Numerous resources described in this section will help you identify actual employers. Use all of them or any others that you identify as available in your geographic area. As you become experienced in this process, you'll quickly figure out which information sources are helpful and which are not. If you live in a rural area, a well-planned day trip to a major city that includes a college career office, a large college or city library, state and federal employment centers, a chamber of commerce office, and a well-stocked bookstore can produce valuable results.

There are many excellent resources available to help you identify actual job sites. They are categorized into employer directories (usually indexed by product lines and geographic location), geographically based directories (designed to highlight particular cities, regions, or states), career-specific directories (e.g., *Sports MarketPlace*, which lists tens of thousands of firms involved with sports), periodicals and newspapers, targeted job posting publications, and videos. This is by no means meant to be a complete treatment of resources but rather a starting point for identifying useful resources.

Working from the more general references to highly specific resources, we provide a basic list to help you begin your search. Many of these you'll find easily available. In some cases reference librarians and others will suggest even better materials for your particular situation. Start to create your own customized bibliography of job search references.

Geographically Based Directories. The Job Bank series published by Bob Adams, Inc. (aip.com) contains detailed entries on each area's major employers, including business activity, address, phone number, and hiring contact name. Many listings specify educational backgrounds being sought in potential employees. Each volume contains a solid discussion of each city's or state's major employment sectors. Organizations are also indexed by industry. Job Bank volumes are available for the following places: Atlanta, Boston, Chicago, Dallas–Ft. Worth, Denver, Detroit, Florida, Houston, Los Angeles, Minneapolis, New York, Ohio, Philadelphia, San Francisco, Seattle, St. Louis, Washington, D.C., and other cities throughout the Northwest.

National Job Bank (careercity.com) lists employers in every state, along with contact names and commonly hired job categories. Included are many small companies often overlooked by other directories. Companies are also indexed by industry. This publication provides information on educational backgrounds sought and lists company benefits.

Periodicals and Newspapers. Several sources are available to help you locate which journals or magazines carry job advertisements in your field. Other resources help you identify opportunities in other parts of the country.

- *Where the Jobs Are: A Comprehensive Directory of 1200 Journals Listing Career Opportunities*
- *Corptech Fast 5000 Company Locator*
- *National Ad Search* (nationaladsearch.com)
- *The Federal Jobs Digest* (jobsfed.com) and *Federal Career Opportunities*
- *World Chamber of Commerce Directory* (chamberofcommerce.org)

This list is certainly not exhaustive; use it to begin your job search work.

Targeted Job Posting Publications. Although the resources that follow are national in scope, they are either targeted to one medium of contact (telephone), focused on specific types of jobs, or less comprehensive than the sources previously listed.

- *Job Hotlines USA* (careers.org/topic/01_002.html)
- *The Job Hunter* (jobhunter.com)
- *Current Jobs for Graduates* (graduatejobs.com)
- *Environmental Opportunities* (ecojobs.com)
- *Y National Vacancy List* (ymcahrm.ns.ca/employed/jobleads.html)
- *ARTSearch*
- *Community Jobs*
- *National Association of Colleges and Employers: Job Choices series*
- *National Association of Colleges and Employers* (naceweb.org)

Videos. You may be one of the many job seekers who likes to get information via a medium other than paper. Many career libraries, public libraries, and career centers in libraries carry an assortment of videos that will help you learn new techniques and get information helpful in the job search.

Locating Information Resources

Throughout these introductory chapters, we have continually referred you to various websites for information on everything from job listings to career information. Using the Web gives you a mobility at your computer that you don't enjoy if you rely solely on books or newspapers or printed journals. Moreover, material on the Web, if the site is maintained, can be the most up-to-date information available.

You'll eventually identify the information resources that work best for you, but make certain you've covered the full range of resources before you begin to rely on a smaller list. Here's a short list of informational sites that many job seekers find helpful:

- Public and college libraries
- College career centers
- Bookstores
- Internet
- Local and state government personnel offices
- Career/job fairs

Each one of these sites offers a collection of resources that will help you get the information you need.

As you meet and talk with service professionals at all these sites, be sure to let them know what you're doing. Inform them of your job search, what you've already accomplished, and what you're looking for. The more people who know you're job seeking, the greater the possibility that someone will have information or know someone who can help you along your way.

4

Interviewing and Job Offer Considerations

Certainly, there can be no one part of the job search process more fraught with anxiety and worry than the interview. Yet seasoned job seekers welcome the interview and will often say, "Just get me an interview and I'm on my way!" They understand that the interview is crucial to the hiring process and equally crucial for them, as job candidates, to have the opportunity of a personal dialogue to add to what the employer may already have learned from the résumé, cover letter, and telephone conversations.

Believe it or not, the interview is to be welcomed, and even enjoyed! It is a perfect opportunity for you, the candidate, to sit down with an employer and express yourself and display who you are and what you want. Of course, it takes thought and planning and a little strategy; after all, it *is* a job interview! But it can be a positive, if not pleasant, experience and one you can look back on and feel confident about your performance and effort.

For many new job seekers, a job, any job, seems a wonderful thing. But seasoned interview veterans know that the job interview is an important step for both sides—the employer and the candidate—to see what each has to offer and whether there is going to be a "fit" of personalities, work styles, and attitudes. And it is this concept of balance in the interview, that both sides have important parts to play, that holds the key to success in mastering this aspect of the job search strategy.

Try to think of the interview as a conversation between two interested and equal partners. You both have important, even vital, information to deliver and to learn. Of course, there's no denying the employer has some leverage, especially in the initial interview for recruitment or any interview scheduled by the candidate and not the recruiter. That should not prevent the interviewee from seeking to play an equal part in what should be a fair exchange of information. Too often the untutored candidate allows the interview to become one-sided. The employer asks all the questions and the candidate simply responds. The ideal would be for two mutually interested parties to sit down and discuss possibilities for each. This is a conversation of significance, and it requires preparation, thought about the tone of the interview, and planning of the nature and details of the information to be exchanged.

Preparing for the Interview

The length of most initial interviews is about thirty minutes. Given the brevity, the information that is exchanged ought to be important. The candidate should be delivering material that the employer cannot discover on the résumé, and in turn, the candidate should be learning things about the employer that he or she could not otherwise find out. After all, if you have only thirty minutes, why waste time on information that is already published? The information exchanged is more than just factual, and both sides will learn much from what they see of each other, as well. How the candidate looks, speaks, and acts are important to the employer. The employer's attention to the interview and awareness of the candidate's résumé, the setting, and the quality of information presented are important to the candidate.

Just as the employer has every right to be disappointed when a prospect is late for the interview, looks unkempt, and seems ill-prepared to answer fairly standard questions, the candidate may be disappointed with an interviewer who isn't ready for the meeting, hasn't learned the basic résumé facts, and is constantly interrupted by telephone calls. In either situation there's good reason to feel let down.

There are many elements to a successful interview, and some of them are not easy to describe or prepare for. Sometimes there is just a chemistry between interviewer and interviewee that brings out the best in both, and a good exchange takes place. But there is much the candidate can do to pave the way for success in terms of his or her résumé, personal appearance, goals, and interview strategy—each of which we will discuss. However, none of this preparation is as important as the time and thought the candidate gives to personal self-assessment.

Self-Assessment

Neither a stunning résumé nor an expensive, well-tailored suit can compensate for candidates who do not know what they want, where they are going, or why they are interviewing with a particular employer. Self-assessment, the process by which we begin to know and acknowledge our own particular blend of education, experiences, needs, and goals, is not something that can be sorted out the weekend before a major interview. Of all the elements of interview preparation, this one requires the longest lead time and cannot be faked.

Because the time allotted for most interviews is brief, it is all the more important for job candidates to understand and express succinctly why they are there and what they have to offer. This is not a time for undue modesty (or for braggadocio either); it is a time for a compelling, reasoned statement of why you feel that you and this employer might make a good match. It means you have to have thought about your skills, interests, and attributes; related those to your life experiences and your own history of challenges and opportunities; and determined what that indicates about your strengths, preferences, values, and areas needing further development.

If you need some assistance with self-assessment issues, refer to Chapter 1. Included are suggested exercises that can be done as needed, such as making up an experiential diary and extracting obvious strengths and weaknesses from past experiences. These simple assignments will help you look at past activities as collections of tasks with accompanying skills and responsibilities. Don't overlook your high school or college career office. Many offer personal counseling on self-assessment issues and may provide testing instruments such as the *Myers-Briggs Type Indicator (MBTI)*, the *Harrington-O'Shea Career Decision-Making System (CDM)*, the *Strong Interest Inventory (SII)*, or any other of a wide selection of assessment tools that can help you clarify some of these issues prior to the interview stage of your job search.

The Résumé

Résumé preparation has been discussed in detail, and some basic examples were provided. In this section we want to concentrate on how best to use your résumé in the interview. In most cases the employer will have seen the résumé prior to the interview, and, in fact, it may well have been the quality of that résumé that secured the interview opportunity.

An interview is a conversation, however, and not an exercise in reading. So, if the employer hasn't seen your résumé and you have brought it along to the interview, wait until asked or until the end of the interview to offer it. Otherwise, you may find yourself staring at the back of your résumé and simply answering "yes" and "no" to a series of questions drawn from that document.

Sometimes an interviewer is not prepared and does not know or recall the contents of the résumé and may use the résumé to a greater or lesser degree as a "prompt" during the interview. It is for you to judge what that may indicate about the individual performing the interview or the employer. If your interviewer seems surprised by the scheduled meeting, relies on the résumé to an inordinate degree, and seems otherwise unfamiliar with your background, this lack of preparation for the hiring process could well be a symptom of general management disorganization or may simply be the result of poor planning on the part of one individual. It is your responsibility as a potential employee to be aware of these signals and make your decisions accordingly.

In any event, it is perfectly acceptable for you to get the conversation back to a more interpersonal style by saying something like, "Mr. Smith, you might be interested in some recent design experience I gained in an internship that is not detailed on my résumé. May I tell you about it?" This can return the interview to two people talking to each other, not one reading and the other responding.

By all means, bring at least one copy of your résumé to the interview. Occasionally, at the close of an interview, an interviewer will express an interest in circulating a résumé to several departments, and you could then offer the copy you brought. Sometimes, an interview appointment provides an opportunity to meet others in the organization who may express an interest in you and your background, and it may be helpful to follow up with a copy of your résumé. Our best advice, however, is to keep it out of sight until needed or requested.

Employer Information

Whether your interview is for graduate school admission, an overseas corporate position, or a position with a local company, it is important to know something about the employer or the organization. Keeping in mind that the interview is relatively brief and that you will hopefully have other interviews with other organizations, it is important to keep your research in proportion. If secondary interviews are called for, you will have additional time to do further research. For the first interview, it is helpful to know the organization's mission, goals, size, scope of operations, and so forth. Your research may uncover recent areas of challenge or particular successes that may help to fuel the interview. Use the "What Do They Call the Job You Want?" section of Chapter 3, your library, and your career or guidance office to help you locate this information in the most efficient way possible. Don't be shy in asking advice of these counseling and guidance professionals on how best to spend your preparation time. With some practice, you'll soon learn how much information is enough and which kinds of information are most useful to you.

Interview Content

We've already discussed how it can help to think of the interview as an important conversation—one that, as with any conversation, you want to find pleasant and interesting and to leave you with a good feeling. But because this conversation is especially important, the information that's exchanged is critical to its success. What do you want them to know about you? What do you need to know about them? What interview technique do you need to particularly pay attention to? How do you want to manage the close of the interview? What steps will follow in the hiring process?

Except for the professional interviewer, most of us find interviewing stressful and anxiety-provoking. Developing a strategy before you begin interviewing will help you relieve some stress and anxiety. One particular strategy that has worked for many and may work for you is interviewing by objective. Before you interview, write down three to five goals you would like to achieve for that interview. They may be technique goals: smile a little more, have a firmer handshake, be sure to ask about the next stage in the interview process before leaving. They may be content-oriented goals: find out about the company's current challenges and opportunities; be sure to speak of your recent research, writing experiences, or foreign travel. Whatever your goals, jot down a few of them as goals for each interview.

Most people find that in trying to achieve these few goals, their interviewing technique becomes more organized and focused. After the interview, the most common question friends and family ask is "How did it go?" With this technique, you have an indication of whether you met *your* goals for the meeting, not just some vague idea of how it went. Chances are, if you accomplished what you wanted to, it improved the quality of the entire interview. As you continue to interview, you will want to revise your goals to continue improving your interview skills.

Now, add to the concept of the significant conversation the idea of a beginning, a middle, and a closing and you will have two thoughts that will give your interview a distinctive character. Be sure to make your introduction warm and cordial. Say your full name (and if it's a difficult-to-pronounce name, help the interviewer to pronounce it) and make certain you know your interviewer's name and how to pronounce it. Most interviews begin with some "soft talk" about the weather, chat about the candidate's trip to the interview site, or national events. This is done as a courtesy to relax both you and the interviewer, to get you talking, and to generally try to defuse the atmosphere of excessive tension. Try to be yourself, engage in the conversation, and don't try to second-guess the interviewer. This is simply what it appears to be—casual conversation.

Once you and the interviewer move on to exchange more serious information in the middle part of the interview, the two most important concerns become your ability to handle challenging questions and your success at asking meaningful ones. Interviewer questions will probably fall into one of three categories: personal assessment and career direction, academic assessment, and knowledge of the employer. Here are a few examples of questions in each category:

Personal Assessment and Career Direction
1. What motivates you to put forth your best effort?
2. What do you consider to be your greatest strengths and weaknesses?
3. What qualifications do you have that make you think you will be successful in this career?

Academic Assessment
1. What led you to choose your major?
2. What subjects did you like best and least? Why?
3. How has your college experience prepared you for this career?

Knowledge of the Employer
1. What do you think it takes to be successful in an organization like ours?
2. In what ways do you think you can make a contribution to our organization?
3. Why did you choose to seek a position with this organization?

The interviewer wants a response to each question but is also gauging your enthusiasm, preparedness, and willingness to communicate. In each response you should provide some information about yourself that can be related to the employer's needs. A common mistake is to give too much information. Answer each question completely, but be careful not to run on too long with extensive details or examples.

Questions About Underdeveloped Skills

Most employers interview people who have met some minimum criteria of education and experience. They interview candidates to see who they are, to learn what kind of personality they exhibit, and to get some sense of how this person might fit into the existing organization. It may be that you are asked about skills the employer hopes to find and that you have not documented. Maybe it's grant-writing experience, knowledge of the European political system, or a knowledge of the film world.

To questions about skills and experiences you don't have, answer honestly and forthrightly and try to offer some additional information about skills you do have. For example, perhaps the employer is disappointed you have no grant-writing experience. An honest answer may be as follows:

No, unfortunately, I was never in a position to acquire those skills. I do understand something of the complexities of the grant-writing process and feel confident that my attention to detail, careful reading skills, and strong writing would make grants a wonderful challenge in a new job. I think I could get up on the learning curve quickly.

The employer hears an honest admission of lack of experience but is reassured by some specific skill details that do relate to grant writing and a confident manner that suggests enthusiasm and interest in a challenge.

For many students, questions about their possible contribution to an employer's organization can prove challenging. Because your education has probably not included specific training for a job, you need to review your academic record and select capabilities you have developed in your major that an employer can appreciate. For example, perhaps you read well and can analyze and condense what you've read into smaller, more focused pieces. That could be valuable. Or maybe you did some serious research and you know you have valuable investigative skills. Your public speaking might be highly developed and you might use visual aids appropriately and effectively. Or maybe your skill at correspondence, memos, and messages is effective. Whatever it is, you must take it out of the academic context and put it into a new, employer-friendly context so your interviewer can best judge how you could help the organization.

Exhibiting knowledge of the organization will, without a doubt, show the interviewer that you are interested enough in the available position to have done some legwork in preparation for the interview. Remember, it is not necessary to know every detail of the organization's history but rather to have a general knowledge about why it is in business and how the industry is faring.

Sometime during the interview, generally after the midway point, you'll be asked if you have any questions for the interviewer. Your questions will tell the employer much about your attitude and your desire to understand the organization's expectations so you can compare them to your own strengths. The following are just a few questions you might want to ask:

1. What is the communication style of the organization? (meetings, memos, and so forth)
2. What would a typical day in this position be like for me?
3. What have been some of the interesting challenges and opportunities your organization has recently faced?

Most interviews draw to a natural closing point, so be careful not to prolong the discussion. At a signal from the interviewer, wind up your presentation, express your appreciation for the opportunity, and be sure to ask what the next stage in the process will be. When can you expect to hear from them? Will they be conducting second-tier interviews? If you are interested and haven't heard, would they mind a phone call? Be sure to collect a business card with the name and phone number of your interviewer. On your way out, you might have an opportunity to pick up organizational literature you haven't seen before.

With the right preparation—a thorough self-assessment, professional clothing, and employer information—you'll be able to set and achieve the goals you have established for the interview process.

Interview Follow-Up

Quite often there is a considerable time lag between interviewing for a position and being hired or, in the case of the networker, between your phone call or letter to a possible contact and the opportunity of a meeting. This can be frustrating. "Why aren't they contacting me?" "I thought I'd get another interview, but no one has telephoned." "Am I out of the running?" You don't know what is happening.

Consider the Differing Perspectives

Of course, there is another perspective—that of the networker or hiring organization. Organizations are complex, with multiple tasks that need to be accomplished each day. Hiring is a discrete activity that does not occur as frequently as other job assignments. The hiring process might have to take second place to other, more immediate organizational needs. Although it may be very important to you, and it is certainly ultimately significant to the employer, other issues such as fiscal management, planning and product development, employer vacation periods, or financial constraints may prevent an organization or individual within that organization from acting on your employment or your request for information as quickly as you or they would prefer.

Use Your Communication Skills

Good communication is essential here to resolve any anxieties, and the responsibility is on you, the job or information seeker. Too many job seekers and networkers offer as an excuse that they don't want to "bother" the organization by writing letters or calling. Let us assure you here and now, once and for all, that if you are troubling an organization by over-communicating, someone will indicate that situation to you quite clearly. If not, you can only assume you are a worthwhile prospect and the employer appreciates being reminded of your availability and interest. Let's look at follow-up practices in the job interview process and the networking situation separately.

Following Up on the Employment Interview

A brief thank-you note following an interview is an excellent and polite way to begin a series of follow-up communications with a potential employer with whom you have interviewed and want to remain in touch. It should be just that—a thank-you for a good meeting. If you failed to mention some fact or experience during your interview that you think might add to your candidacy, you may use this note to do that. However, this should be essentially a note whose overall tone is appreciative and, if appropriate, indicative of a continuing interest in pursuing any opportunity that may exist with that organization. It is one of the few pieces of business correspondence that may be handwritten, but always use plain, good-quality, standard-size paper.

If, however, at this point you are no longer interested in the employer, the thank-you note is an appropriate time to indicate that. You are under no obligation to identify any reason for not continuing to pursue employment with that organization, but if you are so inclined to indicate your professional reasons (pursuing other employers more akin to your interests, looking for greater income production than this employer can provide, a different geographic location), you certainly may. It should not be written with an eye to negotiation, for it will not be interpreted as such.

As part of your interview closing, you should have taken the initiative to establish lines of communication for continuing information about your candidacy. If you asked permission to telephone, wait a week following your thank-you note, then telephone your contact simply to inquire how things are progressing on your employment status. The feedback you receive here should be taken at face value. If your interviewer simply has no information, he or she will tell you so and indicate whether you should call again and when. Don't be discouraged if this should continue over some period of time.

If during this time something occurs that you think improves or changes your candidacy (some new qualification or experience you may have had), including any offers from other organizations, by all means telephone or write to inform the employer about this. In the case of an offer from a competing but less desirable or equally desirable organization, telephone your contact, explain what has happened, express your real interest in the organization, and inquire whether some determination on your employment might be made before you must respond to this other offer. An organization that is truly interested in you may be moved to make a decision about your candidacy. Equally possible is the scenario in which they are not yet ready to make a decision and so advise you to take the offer that has been presented. Again, you have no ethical alternative but to deal with the information presented in a straightforward manner.

When accepting other employment, be sure to contact any employers still actively considering you and inform them of your new job. Thank them graciously for their consideration. There are many other job seekers out there just like you who will benefit from having their candidacy improved when others bow out of the race. Who knows, you might at some future time have occasion to interact professionally with one of the organizations with which you sought employment. How embarrassing it would be to have someone remember you as the candidate who failed to notify them that you were taking a job elsewhere!

In all of your follow-up communications, keep good notes of whom you spoke with, when you called, and any instructions that were given about return communications. This will prevent any misunderstandings and provide you with good records of what has transpired.

Job Offer Considerations

For many recent college graduates, the thrill of their first job and, for some, the most substantial regular income they have ever earned seems an excess of good fortune coming at once. To question that first income or to be critical in any way of the conditions of employment at the time of the initial offer seems like looking a gift horse in the mouth. It doesn't seem to occur to many new hires even to attempt to negotiate any aspect of their first job. And, as many employers who deal with entry-level jobs for recent college graduates will readily confirm, the reality is that there simply isn't much movement in salary available to these new college recruits. The entry-level hire generally does not have an employment track record on a professional level to provide any leverage for negotiation. Real negotiations on salary, benefits, retirement provisions, and so forth come to those with significant employment records at higher income levels.

Of course, the job offer is more than just money. It can be composed of geographic assignment, duties and responsibilities, training, benefits, health and medical insurance, educational assistance, car allowance or company vehicle, and a host of other items. All of this is generally detailed in the formal letter that presents the final job offer. In most cases this is a follow-up to a personal phone call from the employer representative who has been principally responsible for your hiring process.

That initial telephone offer is certainly binding as a verbal agreement, but most firms follow up with a detailed letter outlining the most significant parts of your employment contract. You may, of course, choose to respond immediately at the time of the telephone offer (which would be considered a binding oral contract), but you will also be required to formally answer the letter of offer with a letter of acceptance, restating the salient elements of the employer's description of your position, salary, and benefits. This ensures that both parties are clear on the terms and conditions of employment and remuneration and any other outstanding aspects of the job offer.

Is This the Job You Want?

Most new employees will respond affirmatively in writing, glad to be in the position to accept employment. If you've worked hard to get the offer and the job market is tight, other offers may not be in sight, so you will say, "Yes, I accept!" What is important here is that the job offer you accept be one that does fit your particular needs, values, and interests as you've outlined them in your self-assessment process. Moreover, it should be a job that will not only use your skills and education but also challenge you to develop new skills and talents.

Jobs are sometimes accepted too hastily, for the wrong reasons, and without proper scrutiny by the applicant. For example, an individual might readily accept a sales job only to find the continual rejection by potential clients unendurable. An office worker might realize within weeks the constraints of a desk job and yearn for more activity. Employment is an important part of our lives. It is, for most of our adult lives, our most continuous productive activity. We want to make good choices based on the right criteria.

If you have a low tolerance for risk, a job based on commission will certainly be very anxiety-provoking. If being near your family is important, issues of relocation could present a decision crisis for you. If you're an adventurous person, a job with frequent travel would provide needed excitement and be very desirable. The importance of income, the need to continue your education, your personal health situation—all of these have an impact on whether the job you are considering will ultimately meet your needs. Unless you've spent some time understanding and thinking about these issues, it will be difficult to evaluate offers you do receive.

More important, if you make a decision that you cannot tolerate and feel you must leave that job, you will then have both unemployment and self-esteem issues to contend with. These will combine to make the next job search tough going, indeed. So make your acceptance a carefully considered decision.

Negotiating Your Offer

It may be that there is some aspect of your job offer that is not particularly attractive to you. Perhaps there is no relocation allotment to help you move your possessions, and this presents some financial hardship for you. It may be that the health insurance is less than you had hoped. Your initial assignment may be different from what you expected, either in its location or in the duties and responsibilities that comprise it. Or it may simply be that the salary is less than you anticipated. Other considerations may be your official starting date of employment, vacation time, evening hours, dates of training programs or schools, and other concerns.

If you are considering not accepting the job because of some item or items in the job offer "package" that do not meet your needs, you should know that most employers emphatically wish that you would bring that issue to their attention. It may be that the employer can alter it to make the offer more agreeable for you. In some cases it cannot be changed. In any event the employer would generally like to have the opportunity to try to remedy a difficulty rather than risk losing a good potential employee over an issue that might have been resolved. After all, they have spent time and funds in securing your services, and they certainly deserve an opportunity to resolve any possible differences.

Honesty is the best approach in discussing any objections or uneasiness you might have over the employer's offer. Having received your formal offer in writing, contact your employer representative and indicate your particular dissatisfaction in a straightforward manner. For example, you might explain that while you are very interested in being employed by this organization, the salary (or any other benefit) is less than you have determined you require. State the terms you need, and listen to the response. You may be asked to put this in writing, or you may be asked to hold off until the firm can decide on a response. If you are dealing with a senior representative of the organization, one who has been involved in hiring for some time, you may get an immediate response or a solid indication of possible outcomes.

Perhaps the issue is one of relocation. Your initial assignment is in the Midwest, and because you had indicated a strong West Coast preference, you are surprised at the actual assignment. You might simply indicate that while you understand the need for the company to assign you based on its needs, you are disappointed and had hoped to be placed on the West Coast. You could inquire if that were still possible and, if not, would it be reasonable to expect a West Coast relocation in the future.

If your request is presented in a reasonable way, most employers will not see this as jeopardizing your offer. If they can agree to your proposal, they will. If not, they will simply tell you so, and you may choose to continue your candidacy with them or remove yourself from consideration. The choice will be up to you.

Some firms will adjust benefits within their parameters to meet the candidate's need if at all possible. If a candidate requires a relocation cost allowance, he or she may be asked to forgo tuition benefits for the first year to accomplish this adjustment. An increase in life insurance may be adjusted by some other benefit trade-off; perhaps a family dental plan is not needed. In these decisions you are called upon, sometimes under time pressure, to know how you value these issues and how important each is to you.

Many employers find they are more comfortable negotiating for candidates who have unique qualifications or who bring especially needed expertise to the organization. Employers hiring large numbers of entry-level college graduates may be far more reluctant to accommodate any changes in offer conditions. They are well supplied with candidates with similar education and experience so that if rejected by one candidate, they can draw new candidates from an ample labor pool.

Comparing Offers

The condition of the economy, the job seeker's academic major and particular geographic job market, and individual needs and demands for certain employment conditions may not provide more than one job offer at a time. Some job seekers may feel that no reasonable offer should go unaccepted for the simple fear there won't be another.

In a tough job market, or if the job you seek is not widely available, or when your job search goes on too long and becomes difficult to sustain financially and emotionally, it may be necessary to accept an inferior offer. The alternative is continued unemployment. Even here, when you feel you don't have a choice, you can at least understand that in accepting this particular offer, there may be limitations and conditions you don't appreciate. At the time of acceptance, there were no other alternatives, but you can begin to use that position to gain the experience and talent to move toward a more attractive position.

Sometimes, however, more than one offer is received, and the candidate has the luxury of choice. If the job seeker knows what he or she wants and has done the necessary self-assessment honestly and thoroughly, it may be clear that one of the offers conforms more closely to those expressed wants and needs.

However, if, as so often happens, the offers are similar in terms of conditions and salary, the question then becomes which organization might provide the necessary climate, opportunities, and advantages for your professional development and growth. This is the time when solid employer research and astute questioning during the interviews really pays off. How much did you learn about the employer through your own research and skillful questioning? When the interviewer asked during the interview "Do you have any questions?" did you ask the kinds of questions that would help resolve a choice between one organization and another? Just as an employer must decide among numerous applicants, so must the applicant learn to assess the potential employer. Both are partners in the job search.

Reneging on an Offer

An especially disturbing occurrence for employers and career counseling professionals is when a job seeker formally (either orally or by written contract) accepts employment with one organization and later reneges on the agreement and goes with another employer.

There are all kinds of rationalizations offered for this unethical behavior. None of them satisfies. The sad irony is that what the job seeker is willing to do to the employer—make a promise and then break it—he or she would be outraged to have done to him- or herself: have the job offer pulled. It is a very bad way to begin a career. It suggests the individual has not taken the time to do the necessary self-assessment and self-awareness exercises to think and judge critically. The new offer taken may, in fact, be no better or worse than the one refused. You should be aware that there have been incidents of legal action following job candidates' reneging on an offer. This adds a very sour note to what should be a harmonious beginning of a lifelong adventure.

PART TWO

THE CAREER PATHS

5

Path 1: Teaching Art

"Poor is the pupil who does not surpass his master."
—LEONARDO DA VINCI

The old adage "Those who can, do, those who can't, teach," couldn't be farther from the truth for this particular career path.

For the most part, art educators *can* do as well as teach.

For many, a job as an art teacher is a means to an end. They place their teaching job in a companion role to a parallel or primary career as a studio or commercial artist. The teaching job provides the security of a regular paycheck and health benefits that a freelancing career might not offer—at least yet. Most states have tenure laws that prevent teachers from being fired without just cause and due process. Teachers may obtain tenure after they have satisfactorily completed a probationary period of teaching, normally three years. Tenure is not a guarantee of a job, but it does provide some security.

Full-time art teaching positions in public or private schools are often on ten-month contracts, leaving summers and several weeks during the year free to pursue individual projects. Art teachers can also work part-time in many settings, leaving even more hours free for studio or commercial art undertakings.

For others, teaching is the end to the means. For these teachers, a love of and skill for the subject area is best expressed by sharing it and encouraging others. Although most probably still practice their art, they do it more for self-expression and self-satisfaction than as a way to provide a living.

Some would say that all artists are able to teach, that the ability to share technique and encourage proficiency is a natural extension of their own creativity. This may or may not be true.

However, no matter the subject area—art or science or air-conditioning repair—there are qualities and skills that all teachers must possess. In addition to being knowledgeable in their subject, the ability to communicate, inspire trust and confidence, and motivate students, as well as understand their educational and emotional needs, are essential for teachers. They also should be organized, dependable, and patient, as well as creative.

Definition of the Career Path

In this section, we will look at all the settings in which an art educator can be employed. The range is much wider for art than a subject teacher working in, for example, history or math. The degree of formal training and qualifications also vary depending on the work setting.

Is it necessary to have a college degree to teach art? The answer to that is a resounding "no." In many situations and settings, your skill, as evidenced by your portfolio or reputation, would be highly sought after. The professional artist, who might not have a formal degree but has made a "name" for him- or herself, is often invited as a guest lecturer to teach studio classes or workshops at various art schools or other settings across the country. But this is for the established artist. However, those of you just starting out who have not yet earned a reputation can still find employment without the degree. This employment is generally on a part-time basis, though, usually with an hourly wage for a salary.

To pursue the profession full-time and to earn a professional-level salary, a bachelor's degree is the usual minimum requirement. But is it necessary to have a state teaching certificate to find work as an art teacher? To work in most public school systems, the answer to that question is "yes," although some public school districts make provisions to grant temporary certification to noncredentialed teachers. These districts have had difficulty securing teachers because of location or pay scale. However, this practice is not common.

Some private schools will also hire noncertified teachers, but with the high supply and relatively small demand for art teachers, they, too, often require teachers to have the same credentials the public schools do.

To work in most public school systems, the bachelor's degree with a teaching certification is required. In other settings, such as art schools and colleges, community colleges, and four-year universities, postgraduate degrees may be required.

Possible Employers

Art instructors have a variety of settings from which to choose. Working conditions, pay scales, and the attitude, motivation, and proficiency of the students will vary depending upon the setting. Here is a sampling of the possible avenues to pursue:

- Adult education centers
- Alternative schools
- Art schools
- Private schools
- Public schools
- Community colleges
- Four-year colleges and universities
- Religious organizations
- Museums
- International schools
- Prisons
- Rehabilitation centers
- Group homes
- Halfway houses
- Summer camps
- Recreation centers
- Parks departments
- Community centers
- Discovery centers
- Department of Defense schools

Possible Job Titles

There is not a wide latitude in job title for the professional art teacher. We often apply the term *teacher* to indicate professionals in elementary school as well as the professionals filling the top posts at universities or art colleges.

They are all, to some extent, teachers. To students, the distinctions between the high school art teacher, the adult education instructor, and the university professor might not hold any critical importance. Despite the subject area, rank, or setting, the teaching role essentially remains the same.

Here an art teacher working in a school setting discusses her job.

Lynne Robbins
Lynne Robbins is a special education teacher at the William Monroe Trotter School, an elementary school in Boston. She studied at Bennington College in Vermont and earned her B.A. in psychology with a concentration in

art. She earned her M.Ed. at Boston College in special education and most recently her master's of science in art education (M.S.A.E.), from Massachusetts College of Art in 1996.

"I work with special education children in grades one through five as well as with regular education children in integrated classrooms. I am a certified art teacher, special education teacher, and elementary teacher. I have taught in several fields beginning with multiple handicapped deaf children to adolescents with multiple handicaps and deafness. I then switched to working with disadvantaged children in the inner-city schools.

"I have a background as an artist (mixed media, metals, textbook illustration, and advertising), and most of what I do as a teacher involves the same processes. Teaching is a very creative profession. It involves working with ideas and making them take root in reality. For example, a recent project involved studying solar energy and then creating, painting, and decorating solar cars and solar-powered vehicles.

"A typical day involves working with twenty-two learning handicapped children during six or seven block periods. Most are 'pulled out' from their regular classes; sometimes I work with them in the classroom, along with the entire class.

"The city of Boston, as well as the country, is working with new goals and standards for education. There is a lot of curriculum change, innovation—all the elements that artists love—challenge, innovation, problems to solve, and materials to utilize. I call my work 'creating with a human canvas.'

"Currently, some students are creating books by using disposable cameras, getting prints, creating chapter heads, writing 'pitchlines' of fifteen words or fewer for chapters, editing them for spelling (using process writing procedures), and then binding them into hardcover books. Some students may be doing independent research projects using the Internet on computers that were purchased through arts-based grants.

"The teaching day goes from 9:00 A.M. to 3:30 P.M. I often use time after school to coach students or do an after-school class or project in the district. Workshops are always available for teachers—lots of opportunities for professional growth and development.

"My job is infinitely creative. It is challenging, process-oriented, and unpredictable; one never knows what the next minute or hour might bring.

"The projects, which are arts- or science-based, are creative in scope and thus fascinating for me to develop and implement. I often need to get grants, write them, and have them funded. My school is multicultural—primarily

African-American and Asian—and I enjoy the challenge and pleasures of working with people of various cultural backgrounds.

"Working with children and their parents has brought me a great deal of personal happiness and joy. I can see myself working as an educator forever."

Lynne Robbins's Career Path. "I am an artist. I visited the classroom of a gifted teacher at a Headstart program in Vermont when I was at Bennington. The teacher lacked money but had great ideas: brushes were made from sponges and branches and blocks from lumber scraps and pegs. The children were happy and busy. I thought the teacher was a miracle worker. I wanted to be one, too.

"I fell into my first job through a summer camp job as an art teacher at a behavior-modification camp. I then had a chance encounter with a social worker at a campus lab school for handicapped children. I worked there as a teacher's assistant for a regular class and as an art teacher for the entire school. I'll never forget the day some of the wheelchair kids deliberately tipped over cans of paint and wheeled through them, streaking the corridors with all manner of color tracks. They also grabbed brushes and streaked the walls as they went down the hall. I thought I would die on the spot. I also worked with deaf and multiple handicapped children and adults for nine years. I held jobs in both Massachusetts and California, working with private schools, private programs, and community colleges.

"Then, I burned out and took off about four years to work as a freelancer and ad artist. At the same time, I went back to school to receive certification in art education so that I could work as an art teacher in the public schools. My training and student teaching were exciting; my elementary classes gave me a standing ovation and my high school classes were exhilarating.

"When I learned Boston was looking for teachers, I applied as a special education teacher to get into the system. My assignments were as an elementary moderate special needs teacher. However, my art training was not in vain—most of my projects with students were arts based and received recognition both for the students and myself."

Some Advice from Lynne. "If you want to teach, you will need to reach down deep inside yourself and ask yourself if you have the stamina, commitment, creativity, and endurance.

"The challenge for me has come from the fact that I happen to be deaf and am working with hearing students, which has made for many a hairy and hair-raising experience. It has been a personal journey for me, as well as a professional one—learning to deal with the nature of the beast.

"Teaching has been a struggle for me, because it exposed me to the best and worst of human nature on a daily basis—my own and others! It will call for everything you have. It will demand that you draw on the mental, spiritual, and emotional resources that you didn't even know existed. The payoff will come from knowing that you can make a difference in the lives of many individuals.

"I found it's also important to have good organization skills. You should be able to structure even the most creative of projects, at least externally, because special education students often work best from a structured base, going from structure to creativity.

"Special education students are not the Brady Bunch—you'll need a great deal of patience and tolerance and a sense of humor."

Working Conditions

School Systems

Kindergarten and elementary school teachers play a vital role in the development of children. What children learn and experience during their early years can shape children's views of themselves and the world, and affect later success or failure in school, work, and their personal lives.

Kindergarten and elementary school teachers introduce children to numbers, language, science, and social studies. They may use games, music, artwork, films, slides, computers, and other instructional technology to teach basic skills.

Most elementary school teachers instruct one class of children in several subjects. In some schools, two or more teachers teach as a team and are jointly responsible for a group of students in at least one subject.

In other schools, a teacher may teach one special subject, usually art, music, reading, science, arithmetic, or physical education, to a number of classes. A small but growing number of teachers instruct multilevel classrooms, those with students at several different learning levels.

In addition to classroom activities, teachers plan and evaluate lessons, sometimes in collaboration with teachers of related subjects. They also prepare tests, grade papers, prepare report cards, oversee study halls and homerooms, supervise extracurricular activities, and meet with parents and school staff to discuss a student's academic progress or personal problems.

In recent years, site-based management, which allows teachers and parents to participate actively in management decisions, has gained popularity.

In many schools, teachers help make decisions regarding the budget, personnel, textbook choices, curriculum design, and teaching methods.

Secondary school teachers help students delve more deeply into subjects introduced in elementary school and learn more about the world and about themselves. They specialize in a specific subject, such as art, music, English, Spanish, mathematics, history, or biology, in junior high/middle school or high school. They may teach a variety of related courses, for example, American history, contemporary American problems, and world geography.

Secondary school teachers may assist a student in choosing courses, colleges, and careers. Special education teachers may help students with their transition into special vocational training programs, colleges, or a job. Teachers also participate in education conferences and workshops.

Teachers design their classroom presentations to meet student needs and abilities. They also may work with students individually. Teachers assign lessons, give tests, hear oral presentations, and maintain classroom discipline.

Teachers observe and evaluate a student's performance and potential. Teachers increasingly are using new assessment methods, such as examining a portfolio of a student's artwork or writing to measure student achievement. Teachers assess the portfolio at the end of a learning period to judge a student's overall progress. They may then provide additional assistance in areas where a student may need help.

Seeing students develop new skills and gain an appreciation of the joy of learning can be very rewarding.

Art Schools, Colleges, and Universities

Generally, faculty are organized into departments or divisions, based on subject or field. They usually teach several different courses in their department, for example, in a B.F.A. program, an art instructor might teach courses in oil painting, pastels, and watercolors. They may instruct undergraduate or graduate students, or both.

In art schools or colleges, faculty may work with small groups in studio classes or give lectures on art history or other areas to several hundred students in large halls. They also grade and evaluate assignments and projects and advise and work with students individually. In universities, they also counsel, advise, teach, and supervise graduate student research.

Most faculty members serve on academic or administrative committees that deal with the policies of their institution, departmental matters, academic issues, curricula, budgets, equipment purchases, and hiring. Some work with student organizations. Department heads generally have heavier administrative responsibilities.

The amount of time spent on each of these activities varies by individual circumstance and type of institution. Faculty members at universities generally spend a significant part of their time doing research; those in four-year colleges, somewhat less; and those in two-year colleges, relatively little. However, the teaching load usually is heavier in two-year colleges.

College faculty generally have flexible schedules. They must be present for classes, usually twelve to sixteen hours a week, and for faculty and committee meetings. Most establish regular office hours for student consultations, usually three to six hours per week. Otherwise, they are relatively free to decide when and where they will work, and how much time to devote to course preparation, evaluating student progress, study, research, and other activities.

They may work staggered hours and teach classes at night and on weekends, particularly those faculty who teach older students who may have full-time jobs or family responsibilities on weekdays. They have even greater flexibility during the summer and school holidays, when they may teach or do research, travel, or pursue nonacademic interests.

Adult Education

Art teachers working in adult education have a variety of settings from which to choose. They are employed by public school systems; community and junior colleges; universities; businesses that provide formal education and training for their employees; art and photography schools and institutes; job training centers; community organizations; and recreational facilities such as the YMCA and religious organizations such as neighborhood Jewish Community Centers.

Many adult education teachers work part-time. To accommodate students who may have job or family responsibilities, many courses are offered at night or on weekends, and range from two- to four-hour workshops and one-day minisessions to semester-long courses.

Because adult education teachers work with adult students, they do not encounter some of the behavioral or social problems sometimes found when teaching younger students. The adults are there by choice and usually are highly motivated, attributes that can make teaching these students rewarding and satisfying.

Training and Qualifications

Kindergarten and Elementary

Traditional education programs for kindergarten and elementary school teachers include courses designed specifically for those preparing to teach in the specific subject areas, such as art, music, or mathematics, as well as prescribed professional education courses, such as philosophy of education, psychology of learning, and teaching methods,

Secondary
Aspiring secondary school teachers either major in art as the subject they plan to teach while also taking education courses, or major in education and take art courses as their subject.

Alternative Teacher Certification
Many states offer alternative teacher certification programs for people who have college training in the subject they will teach but do not have the necessary education courses required for a regular certificate. Alternative certification programs were originally designed to ease teacher shortages in certain subjects, such as mathematics and science. The programs have expanded to attract other people into teaching, including recent college graduates and mid-career changers. In some programs, individuals begin teaching immediately under provisional certification. After working under the close supervision of experienced educators for one or two years while taking education courses outside school hours, they receive regular certification if they have progressed satisfactorily.

Under other programs, college graduates who do not meet certification requirements take only those courses that they lack and then become certified. This may take one or two semesters of full-time study.

Aspiring teachers who need certification may also enter programs that grant a master's degree in education, as well as certification. States also issue emergency certificates to individuals who do not meet all requirements for a regular certificate when schools cannot hire enough teachers with regular certificates.

Competency Testing
Almost all states require applicants for teacher certification to be tested for competency in basic skills such as reading and writing, teaching skills, or subject matter proficiency. Almost all require continuing education for renewal of the teacher's certificate; some require a master's degree.

Reciprocity
Many states have reciprocity agreements that make it easier for teachers certified in one state to become certified in another. Teachers may become board certified by successfully completing the National Board for Professional Teaching Standards certification process. This certification is voluntary, but may result in a higher salary.

Information on certification requirements and approved teacher training institutions is available from local school systems and state departments of education.

Colleges and Universities

Most college and university faculty are in four academic ranks: professor, associate professor, assistant professor, and instructor. A small number are lecturers.

Most faculty members are hired as instructors or assistant professors. Four-year colleges and universities generally hire doctoral degree holders for full-time, tenure-track positions, but may hire master's degree holders or doctoral candidates for certain disciplines, such as the arts, or for part-time and temporary jobs.

Doctoral programs usually take four to seven years of full-time study beyond the bachelor's degree. Candidates usually specialize in a subfield of a discipline, for example, European art history, but also take courses covering the whole discipline. Programs include twenty or more increasingly specialized courses and seminars plus comprehensive examinations on all major areas of the field. They also include a dissertation, a report on original research to answer some significant question in the field.

Students in the natural sciences and engineering usually do laboratory work; or they study original documents and other published material. The dissertation, done under the guidance of one or more faculty advisors, usually takes one or two years of full-time work.

Adult Education

Training requirements vary widely by state and by subject. In general, teachers need work or other experience in their field and a license or certificate in fields where these usually are required for full professional status.

In some cases, particularly at educational institutions, a bachelor's, master's, or doctoral degree is required, especially to teach courses that can be applied toward a four-year degree program. In other cases, an acceptable portfolio of work is required. For example, to secure a job teaching a flower-arranging course, an applicant would need to show examples of previous work.

Adult education teachers update their skills through continuing education to maintain certification; requirements vary among institutions. Teachers may take part in seminars, conferences, or graduate courses in adult education, training and development, or human resources development.

Adult education teachers should communicate and relate well with students, enjoy working with them, and be able to motivate them.

Advancement

With additional preparation and certification, teachers may become administrators or supervisors, although the number of positions is limited. In some systems, highly qualified, experienced teachers can become senior or mentor teachers, with higher pay and additional responsibilities. They guide and assist less experienced teachers while keeping most of their teaching responsibilities.

Some faculty, based on teaching experience, research, publication, and service on campus committees and task forces move into administrative and managerial positions, such as departmental chairperson, dean, and president. At four-year institutions, such advancement requires a doctoral degree.

Strategies for Finding the Jobs

College Career Placement Centers

Check with your college career office. Career offices regularly receive mailings of job openings. You can also leave your résumé on file there. Prospective employers regularly contact college career offices looking for likely candidates.

Help Wanted Ads

Seek out all newspapers in your area or in the geographic location in which you'd prefer to work. A trip to the library will reveal periodicals you might not have been aware of and will be less of a burden on your budget.

The Internet

This is an incredible source for job hunting. Use any of the search engines available to you and type in key words such as *employment, art, teaching,* and *jobs.* You will discover a wealth of information online—organizations, educational institutions, publications, and a wide variety of potential employers and job-search services such as monster.com—most of which are available to you at no charge above the service fee your Internet provider charges you.

Internships and Volunteering

Art educators, especially those hoping to land a museum job, will find internships and volunteering stints to be the most important keys in that particular setting. Museums cry out for volunteer help and internships can be arranged through your university. Once in the door, make yourself indispensable. When a job opening occurs, you'll be there on the spot, ready to step in.

Direct Contact

Walk right in and set your portfolio or résumé down on the appropriate desk. You might find you have just landed yourself a job. This approach works best in adult education centers, community centers, and other related settings, as listed under "Possible Employers" earlier in this chapter.

The Chronicle of Higher Education

This is the old standby for those seeking positions within two- and four-year colleges and universities. It is a weekly publication available by subscription or in any library or your college placement office.

Placement Agencies

For private schools particularly, both at home and abroad, placement agencies can provide a valuable source for finding employment. Some charge both the employer and the prospective employee a fee, others charge just one or the other.

Career Outlook

School Systems

According to the *Occupational Outlook Handbook*, compiled by the U.S. Department of Labor, job opportunities for teachers over the next ten years should be excellent, attributable mostly to the large number of teachers expected to retire. Although employment of preschool, kindergarten, elementary, middle, and secondary school teachers is expected to increase about as fast as the average for all occupations, a large proportion will be eligible to retire by 2010, creating many vacancies, particularly at the secondary school level. Intense competition for good teachers is already under way among employers in many locations, with schools luring teachers from other states and districts with bonuses and higher pay.

Overall enrollments through 2010, a key factor in the demand for teachers, are projected to rise slowly, resulting in average employment growth for all teachers from preschool to secondary grades. However, projected enrollments vary by region. States in the south and west—particularly California, Texas, Arizona, and Georgia—will experience large enrollment increases, while states in the northeast and midwest may experience declines. Projected enrollments also differ by grade, with enrollments rising moderately in grades 9 through 12, while remaining fairly steady for all other grades over the 2000–10 period.

The job market for teachers also continues to vary by school location and by subject specialty. Many inner cities—often characterized by overcrowded, ill-equipped schools and higher-than-average poverty rates—and rural areas—characterized by their remote location and relatively low salaries—have difficulty attracting enough teachers, so job prospects should be better in these areas than in suburban districts.

Specialties that currently have an adequate number of qualified teachers include general elementary education, physical education, and social studies. Teachers who are geographically mobile and who obtain licensure in more than one subject should have a distinct advantage in finding a job. Increasing enrollments of minorities, coupled with a shortage of minority teachers, should cause efforts to recruit minority teachers to intensify. Also, the number of non-English-speaking students has grown dramatically, especially in California and Florida, which have large Spanish-speaking student populations, creating demand for bilingual teachers and those who teach English as a second language.

The number of teachers employed also is dependent on state and local expenditures for education and enactment of legislation to increase the quality of education. A number of initiatives, such as reduced class size (primarily in the early elementary grades), mandatory preschool for four-year-olds, and all-day kindergarten have been implemented in a few states, but implementation nationwide has been limited. Additional teachers, particularly preschool and early elementary school teachers, will be needed if states or localities implement any of these measures.

Because of a shortage of teachers in certain locations and in anticipation of the loss of a number of teachers to retirement, many states are implementing policies that will encourage more students to become teachers. Some are giving large signing bonuses that are distributed over the teacher's first few years of teaching. Some are expanding state scholarships; issuing loans for moving expenses; and implementing loan-forgiveness programs, allowing education majors with at least a B average to receive state-paid tuition as long as they agree to teach in the state for four years.

The supply of teachers also is expected to increase in response to reports of improved job prospects, more teacher involvement in school policy, and greater public interest in education. In recent years, the total number of bachelor's and master's degrees granted in education has steadily increased. In addition, more teachers will be drawn from a reserve pool of career changers, substitute teachers, and teachers completing alternative certification programs, relocating to different schools, and reentering the workforce.

Higher Education

The job outlook for postsecondary teachers should be much brighter than it has been in recent years. Employment is expected to grow faster than the average for all occupations through 2010. Projected growth in college and university enrollment over the next decade stems largely from the expected increase in the population of eighteen to twenty-four-year-olds. Adults returning to college and an increase in foreign-born students also will add to the number of students, particularly in the fastest growing states of California, Texas, Florida, New York, and Arizona. Because many of the students will be from minority groups, demand for minority teachers will be high.

Welfare-to-work policies and the growing need to regularly update one's skills will continue to create new opportunities for postsecondary teachers, particularly at community colleges. There also is expected to be a large number of openings because of the retirements of faculty who were hired in the late 1960s and 1970s to teach the baby boomers. In contrast, the number of doctorate degrees is projected to rise by only 4 percent over the 2000–10 period, which is sharply lower than the increase over the previous decade. A surplus of Ph.D. candidates in recent years has contributed to intense competition for college faculty jobs.

Although the competition for jobs should ease somewhat, it will remain tight for those seeking tenure-track positions at four-year colleges and universities. Many of the jobs opening up are expected to be part-time or renewable, term appointments. The best job prospects will continue to be in the computer sciences, engineering, and business fields in which jobs outside academia are plentiful. Vocational-technical education teachers also are in short supply in the computer, business, and health-related fields.

Distance learning, particularly over the Internet, is expected to create a number of new jobs for postsecondary teachers, as this method of education reaches students who would not be able to attend a traditional classroom. Those in rural areas and with family responsibilities are embracing distance education as a way to get the education they want, while minimizing the commute to a campus. In addition, employers are expected to use distance learning as a way to update their employees' skills. The army has recently announced plans to offer distance learning to its troops. Increasing demand for distance education will result in the need for more teachers of online classes, both at traditional colleges and universities and at new online universities.

Adult Education

Opportunities for jobs as self-enrichment education teachers, including art, are expected to be very good. Employment is expected to grow about as fast as the average for all occupations through 2010, and a large number of job openings are also expected because of the need to replace people who leave the occupation or retire. Turnover is prevalent in this occupation because of its many part-time jobs. In addition, a large number of all types of teachers are expected to retire. Should a shortage of people seeking to enter the teaching profession arise, many of these jobs will be hard to fill.

Much of the growth in employment will be for ESL teachers who will be needed by the increasing number of immigrants and other non-English speakers entering this country.

As the baby boomers begin to retire and have more time to take classes and as more people embrace lifelong learning, the need for self-enrichment teachers will grow. Subjects that are not easily researched on the Internet and those that provide hands-on experiences will be in greater demand. Classes on spirituality and self-improvement are expected to be popular along with courses that provide hands-on experiences, like cooking and the arts. Topics related to current trends are always well received.

Earnings

School Systems

According to the American Federation of Teachers, beginning teachers with a bachelor's degree earned an average of $27,989 in the 1999–2000 school year (the most recent figures available). The estimated average salary of all public elementary and secondary school teachers in the 1999–2000 school year was $41,820. The lowest 10 percent earned $23,320 to $28,460; the top 10 percent earned $57,590 to $64,920. Median earnings for preschool teachers were $17,810. Private school teachers generally earn less than public school teachers.

Teachers can boost their salary in a number of ways. In some schools, teachers receive extra pay for coaching sports and working with students in extracurricular activities. Getting a master's degree or national certification often results in a raise in pay, as does acting as a mentor teacher. Some teachers earn extra income during the summer teaching summer school or performing other jobs in the school system.

Higher Education

Median annual earnings of postsecondary teachers in 2000 were $46,330. The middle 50 percent earned between $32,270 and $66,460. The lowest 10 percent earned less than $21,700; the highest 10 percent, more than $87,850.

Earnings for college faculty vary according to rank and type of institution, geographic area, and field. According to a 1999–2000 survey by the American Association of University Professors, salaries for full-time faculty averaged $58,400.

By rank, the averages are as follows:

Professors	$76,200
Associate professors	$55,300
Assistant professors	$45,600
Lecturers	$38,100
Instructors	$34,700

Faculty in four-year institutions earn higher salaries, on average, than do those in two-year schools. In 1999–2000, average salaries for faculty in public institutions ($57,700) were lower than those in private independent institutions ($66,300) but higher than those in religiously-affiliated private colleges and universities ($51,300). In fields with high-paying nonacademic alternatives—medicine, law, engineering, and business, among others—earnings exceed these averages. In others—such as the humanities and education—they are lower.

Most faculty members have significant earnings in addition to their base salary, from consulting, teaching additional courses, research, writing for publication, or other employment.

In addition to typical benefits, most college and university faculty enjoy some unique benefits, including access to campus facilities, tuition waivers for dependents, housing and travel allowances, and paid sabbatical leaves. Part-time faculty usually have fewer benefits than do full-time faculty.

Adult Education

Self-enrichment teachers are generally paid by the hour or the class. Median hourly earnings of self-enrichment teachers were $13.44 in 2000. The middle 50 percent earned between $9.48 and $18.63. The lowest 10 percent earned less than $6.96, and the highest 10 percent earned more than $25.38.

Related Occupations

School Systems

Kindergarten and school teaching requires a wide variety of skills and aptitudes, including a talent for working with children; organizational, administrative, and record-keeping abilities; research and communication skills; the power to influence, motivate, and train others; patience; and creativity. Workers in other occupations requiring some of these aptitudes include college and university faculty, counselors, education administrators, employment interviewers, librarians, preschool workers, public relations specialists, sales representatives, social workers, and trainers and employee development specialists.

Special education teachers work with students with disabilities and special needs. Other occupations that help people with disabilities include school psychologists, speech pathologists, and occupational, physical, and recreational therapists.

Colleges and Universities

College and university faculty function both as teachers and researchers. They communicate information and ideas. Related occupations include elementary and secondary school teachers, librarians, writers, consultants, lobbyists, trainers and employee development specialists, and policy analysts.

Adult Education

Adult education teaching requires a wide variety of skills and aptitudes, including the power to influence, motivate, and train others; organizational, administrative, and communication skills; and creativity. Workers in other occupations that require these aptitudes include other teachers, counselors, school administrators, public relations specialists, employee development specialists and interviewers, and social workers.

Professional Associations

Information on teachers' unions and education-related issues may be obtained from:

American Federation of Teachers
555 New Jersey Avenue NW
Washington, DC 20001
aft.org

National Education Association
1201 16th Street NW
Washington, DC 20036
nea.org

A list of institutions with teacher education programs accredited by the National Council for Accreditation of Teacher Education can be obtained from:

National Council for Accreditation of Teacher Education
2010 Massachusetts Avenue NW, 2nd Floor
Washington, DC 20036
ncate.org

For information on voluntary teacher certification requirements, contact:

National Board for Professional Teaching Standards
1525 Wilson Boulevard
Suite 500
Arlington, VA 22209
nbpts.org

A list of institutions offering training programs in special education may be obtained from:

Council for Exceptional Children
1110 North Glebe Road
Arlington, VA 22201
cec.sped.org

For additional information contact:

American Association for Adult and Continuing Education
1200 19th Street NW, Suite 300
Washington, DC 20036
infolit.org/members/aaace.htm

American Association of Christian Schools
P.O. Box 1097
Independence, MO 64051-0597
aacs.org

American Association of Colleges for Teacher Education
1307 New York Avenue NW, Suite 300
Washington, DC 20005-4701
aacte.org

American Association for Higher Education
One Dupont Circle NW, Suite 360
Washington, DC 20036
aahe.org

**American Association of State Colleges
and Universities**
1307 New York Avenue NW, 5th Floor
Washington, DC 20005
aascu.org

Association of American Colleges and Universities
1818 R Street NW
Washington, DC 20009
aacu-cdu.org

Association for Childhood Education International
17904 Georgia Avenue, Suite 215
Olney, MD 20832
udel.edu/bateman/acei

College Art Association
275 Seventh Avenue
New York, NY 10001
collegeart.org

Council for American Private Education
13017 Wisteria Drive, #457
Germantown, MD 20874
capenet.org

**Kennedy Center Alliance for Arts
Education Network**
2700 F Street NW
Washington, DC 20566
kennedy-center.org/education/kcaaen

National Art Education Association
1916 Association Drive
Reston, VA 20191-1590
naea-reston.org

National Association for the Education of Young Children
1509 16th Street NW
Washington, DC 20019
naeyc.org

National Association of Independent Schools
1620 L Street NW, Suite 1100
Washington, DC 20036-5695
nais.org

National Endowment for the Arts
1100 Pennsylvania Avenue NW
Washington, DC 20506
http://arts.endow.gov

National Independent Private Schools Association
10134 SW 78th Court
Miami, FL 33156
nipsa.org

6

Path 2: Visual Arts

"There are painters who transform the sun into a yellow spot, but there are others who, thanks to their art and intelligence, transform a yellow spot into the sun."
—PABLO PICASSO

Your artistic talent has been practiced and honed through your art degree program and through your own hard work. Your goal has always been to support yourself as an artist or craftsperson, perhaps even to open your own studio, a place in which to create and sell your work. Whether it's pottery or painting, sewing or stained glass, art majors can make a name for themselves and work full-time in their chosen area—without necessarily starving in an artist's garret.

Having said that, few studio artists can move immediately into a career that provides adequate financial support, at least initially. It takes time to build a reputation or a clientele, and during those "lean years," many artists seek out additional avenues where they can be assured of a regular paycheck.

Although some artists might fall into a variety of moonlighting occupations—anything from food service to secretarial work—the vast majority choose to stay in related fields. Those with a teaching certification may teach art in elementary or secondary schools, while those with a master's or Ph.D. degree may teach in colleges or universities.

Some fine artists work in arts administration in city, state, or federal arts programs. Others may work as art critics, art consultants, or as directors or representatives in fine art galleries; give private art lessons; or as curators setting up art exhibits in museums. You will find talented artists working in a variety of settings, many of which are covered in later chapters in this book.

For the serious studio artist, the main goal is to create a work of art that combines and allows for the need for self-expression and the need to make a living. It can be done.

Fine artists advance as their work circulates and as they establish a reputation for a particular style. The best artists continue to grow in ideas, and their work constantly evolves over time.

Definition of the Career Path

Visual artists, which include studio (or fine) artists, graphic artists, and illustrators, use an almost limitless variety of methods and materials to communicate ideas, thoughts, and feelings. They use oils, watercolors, acrylics, pastels, magic markers, pencils, pen and ink, silkscreen, plaster, clay, or any of a number of other media, including computers, to create realistic and abstract works or images of objects, people, nature, topography, or events.

The categories in which visual artists are usually placed depend not so much on the medium, but on the artist's purpose in creating a work of art. Fine artists often create art to satisfy their own need for self-expression and may display their work in museums, corporate collections, art galleries, and private homes. Some of their work may be done on request from clients, but not as exclusively as that of graphic artists.

Studio artists usually work independently, choosing whatever subject matter and medium that suits them. Usually, they specialize in one or two forms of art.

Painters generally work with two-dimensional art forms. Using techniques of shading, perspective, and color-mixing, painters produce works that depict realistic scenes or may evoke different moods and emotions, depending on the artist's goals.

Sculptors design three-dimensional artworks either by molding or joining materials such as clay, glass, wire, plastic, or metal, or cutting and carving forms from a block of plaster, wood, or stone. Some sculptors combine various materials such as concrete, metal, wood, plastic, and paper.

Potters work with a variety of clay materials—from low-fire clays to high-fire stoneware or porcelain—and either hand build their artwork or create different forms using a potter's wheel. They follow existing glaze recipes or experiment with different chemicals to formulate their own.

Printmakers create printed images from designs cut into wood, stone, or metal, or from computer driven data. The designs may be engraved, as in the case of woodblocking; etched as in the production of etchings; or derived from computers in the form of inkjet or laser prints.

Stained-glass artists work with glass, paints, leading, wood, and other materials to create functional as well as decorative artwork such as windows, skylights, or doors.

Photographers use their cameras, lenses, film, and darkroom chemicals the way a painter uses paint and canvas. They capture realistic scenes of people, places, and events, or through the use of various techniques, both natural and contrived, they create photographs that elicit a variety of moods and emotions.

There are myriad other art and craft forms, and a word should be said here about the prudence of combining the two in a book dedicated to art majors. Some would debate whether "crafts" are true art; a long tradition of snobbery has aimed to separate the two forms. However, opportunities for the serious quilter, basketweaver, woodworker, and all the other artisans who work with their hands to create pleasing and commercially accepted works of art have as much place in this book as opportunities for the fine painter or sculptor.

Possible Employers

Although most fine artists are usually self-employed working in their own studios, they still depend on stores, galleries, museums, and private collectors as outlets for their work. Others have what many consider to be the ideal situation—a working studio and storefront combined. Still others follow the art-fair circuit and pack up their artwork and tour the country on a regular basis, deriving most if not all of their income from this source alone.

However, many artists will tell you that any of the above options can be risky, with no guarantee of sales. The art-fair circuit, in particular, can be unreliable, vulnerable to the vagaries of the weather and the whim of impulse buyers or true art lovers and collectors.

For those who prefer the stability of job security and a dependable income, another setting should be noted where artists and artisans may perform their art and be gainfully employed while they do so, either in a full- or part-time capacity.

Living History Museums
A living history museum is a vibrant, active village, town, or city where the day-to-day life of a particular time period has been authentically re-created. Once you step through the gates, you leave the present behind. The houses and public buildings are restored originals or thoroughly researched reproductions. Interiors are outfitted with period furniture, cookware, bed linens, and tablecloths. Peek under a bed and you might even find a two- or three-hundred-year-old mousetrap.

Residents wear the clothing of their day and discuss their dreams and concerns with visitors as they go about their daily tasks. If you were to stop a costumed gentleman passing by and ask where the nearest McDonald's is, he wouldn't have any idea what you were talking about—unless he thought to direct you to a neighbor's farm. He might even do so using the dialect of his home country.

Colonial Williamsburg in Virginia and Plimoth Plantation in Massachusetts are just two examples of living history museums. Addresses of these and several others can be found at the end of this chapter.

These large enterprises offer employment for professional and entry level workers in a wide variety of categories. Those positions that would be of particular interest to art majors are artisans in the historic trades and costumers.

Artisans. Most living history museums employ skilled artisans to demonstrate early crafts and trades. Some of these artisans perform in the first-person, playing the role of a particular character of the time. Others wear modern clothing and discuss their craft from a modern perspective.

In the stores and workshops lining the Duke of Gloucester and Francis Streets in Colonial Williamsburg you will find harness makers, milliners, tailors, needleworkers, silversmiths, apothecaries, candlemakers, bookbinders, printers, and wig makers. Coopers, blacksmiths, joiners (cabinetmakers), potters, basket makers, and weavers are in the Pilgrim Village and Crafts Center at Plimoth Plantation.

In addition to demonstrations, artisans often produce many of the items used on display in the various exhibits. This includes the furniture, cookware, and even sometimes the actual buildings.

Interpretive Artisans at Plimoth Plantation. Most of the items the pilgrims used in 1627 were brought with them on the *Mayflower* or imported later. Because the Pilgrim Village at Plimoth Plantation is time-specific to the year 1627, only those crafts that were practiced then are demonstrated there. In addition to their principal occupation as farmers, 1627 pilgrims were coopers, blacksmiths, thatchers, and house builders. The interpretive artisans perform in costume and play the role of a designated pilgrim documented to have lived in Plymouth during that year.

Deb Mason: A Potter in the Crafts Center. In the Crafts Center at Plimoth Plantation, four different potters demonstrate the art of seventeenth-century throwing techniques, though only one potter is on duty at a time. They also make all the pieces that are used in the Village by the interpreters. During the winter months when the museum is closed to visitors, the potters make enough items to replenish their stock.

In addition to her own home studio, where she teaches pottery classes, does commission work, and makes pieces for display at various galleries, Deb Mason spends two eight-hour days a week in the Crafts Center and is the supervisor of the other potters.

Says Deb, "Back then, the pottery was thrown hastily. There's a real earthy quality to the pieces. Their perception of what was beautiful and what was utilitarian was different from ours. What they strove for was extremely rough by today's standards.

"My biggest problem is remembering not to throw too well. The advantage to that, though, for potters wanting to work here, is that a high degree of skill is not necessary."

Deb Mason's Background. Deb Mason earned her B.A. in art with a major in ceramics in 1973 from Bennington College in Vermont. She taught ceramics full time for thirteen years at a private school and was the head of the art department her last few years there. She joined the staff at Plimoth Plantation in 1992.

Patricia Baker: A Costumer at Plimoth Plantation. Most living history museums employ professional costumers to keep their character interpreters and presenters outfitted in authentic period clothing. Costumers generally work behind the scenes reproducing the apparel the average inhabitant would have worn.

Patricia Baker is wardrobe and textiles manager at Plimoth Plantation, a living history museum that has re-created the year 1627, seven years after the arrival of the *Mayflower* at Plymouth Rock. Her office and workspace occupy a section of a converted dairy barn on the grounds of the museum. The atmosphere is that of a cozy living room with lots of shelves and fabrics draped here and there, sewing machines and rocking chairs, a large cutting table, garment racks, and a radio.

Patricia discusses her job:

"We use wool and linen and a little cotton, all naturally dyed. We try to duplicate the same materials used in the seventeenth century, as well as the same construction techniques. Much of the sewing is done by hand.

"We also make all the household furnishings that are used for display in the various exhibits. These are the seventeenth-century equivalents to what we have in the twenty-first century: sheets, pillowcases (called pillow beres), feather and straw beds, paneled bed curtains, tablecloths and napkins, and cupboard cloths.

"Maintaining and repairing existing costumes and furnishings are also part of our duties, as well as conducting as much research as possible to keep our creations accurate for the particular time period."

Patricia Baker's Background. Patricia graduated from the Massachusetts College of Art in 1976 with a B.F.A. degree (bachelor of fine arts) in crafts. Her concentration was in fabrics and fibers.

She immediately began work at Plimoth Plantation as a character interpreter. In 1985 she joined the wardrobe department and became its head the following year.

Job Strategies for Living History Museums. The competition is fairly high for artisan or costumer positions at a living history museum. For example, the wardrobe department at Plimoth Plantation is a small one, currently employing only four workers. Other larger living history museums, such as Colonial Williamsburg, need more people. A good way to get a foot in the door is to apply for an apprenticeship, internship, or work-study position. Many start out as character interpreters or presenters, then move into their chosen position when openings occur.

Working Conditions

Artists generally work in art and design studios located in commercial space or in their own home studio. Some artists prefer to work alone; others prefer the stimulation of other artists nearby. For the latter group, sharing space with other artists is often a viable alternative to the private studio—both for stimulation and for economics. The trend, in many large cities and even in more out of the way areas as well, is toward shared space in cooperatively owned studios or in rented space in converted warehouses or storefronts.

While artists generally require well-lighted and ventilated surroundings, some art forms create odors and dust from glues, paint, ink, clay, or other materials.

Training and Qualifications

In the fine arts field, formal training requirements do not exist, but it is very difficult to become skilled enough to make a living without some basic training. Bachelor's and graduate degree programs in fine arts are offered in many colleges and universities.

In addition to the skills learned or honed, art majors make important contacts during their formal training years. Instructors are often working artists with hands-on experience and advice to offer.

Career Outlook

Employment of artists and related workers is expected to grow as fast as the average for all occupations through the year 2010. Because the arts attract many talented people with creative ability, the number of aspiring artists continues to grow. Consequently, competition for both salaried jobs and freelance work in some areas is expected to be keen.

Fine artists mostly work on a freelance, or commission, basis and may find it difficult to earn a living solely by selling their artwork. Only the most successful fine artists receive major commissions for their work. Competition among artists for the privilege of being shown in galleries is expected to remain acute. And grants from sponsors such as private foundations, state and local arts councils, and the National Endowment for the Arts, should remain competitive. Nonetheless, studios, galleries, and individual clients are always on the lookout for artists who display outstanding talent, creativity, and style. Population growth, rising incomes, and growth in the number of people who appreciate the fine arts will contribute to the demand for fine artists. Talented fine artists who have developed a mastery of artistic techniques and skills, including computer skills, will have the best job prospects.

Earnings

Median annual earnings of salaried fine artists, including painters, sculptors, and illustrators were $31,190 in 2000. The middle 50 percent earned between $20,460 and $42,720. The lowest 10 percent earned less than $14,690, and the highest 10 percent earned more than $58,580.

The gallery and artist predetermine how much each earns from a sale. Only the most successful fine artists are able to support themselves solely through sale of their works, however. Most fine artists hold other jobs as well.

Earnings for self-employed artists vary widely. Some charge only a nominal fee while they gain experience and build a reputation for their work. Others, such as well-established freelance fine artists and illustrators, can earn more than salaried artists. Many, however, find it difficult to rely solely on income earned from selling paintings or other works of art. Like other self-employed workers, freelance artists must provide their own benefits.

Salaries for artisans within living history museums differ, depending on whether they are full-time or part-time. The latter group earns an hourly wage ranging between $7.50 and $10. A new graduate just starting out full-time could expect to earn in the high-teens to mid-twenties, depending on the location and available funding.

Related Occupations

Workers in other occupations that apply visual art skills are architects, display workers, floral designers, industrial designers, interior designers, landscape architects, and magazine and newspaper layout artists.

Professional Associations

American Arts Alliance
805 15th Street NW, Suite 500
Washington, DC 20005
americanartsalliance.org

American Craft Council
Information Center
72 Spring Street
New York, NY 10012-4019
craftcouncil.org

American Society for Aesthetics
404 Cudahy Hall
Marquette University
Milwaukee, WI 53201-1881
aesthetics-online.org

American Society of Interior Designers
608 Massachusetts Avenue NE
Washington, DC 20002-6006
asid.org

American Society of Media Photographers, Inc.
150 North Second Street
Philadelphia, PA 19106
asmp.org

American Society of Portrait Artists
2781 Zelda Road
Montgomery, AL 36106
asopa.com

**Association for Living Historical Farms and
    Agricultural Museums**
Judith Sheridan, Secretary/Treasurer
8774 Route 45 NW
North Bloomfield, OH 44450
alhfam.org/welcome

**Canadian Association of Photographers and Illustrators in
    Communications**
100 Broadview Avenue, Suite 322
Toronto, ON M4M 3H3
Canada
capic.org/index

The Canadian Association for Photographic Art
31858 Hopedale Avenue
Clearbrook, BC V2T 2G7
Canada
http://capa-acap.ca

Costume Society of America
55 Edgewater Drive
P.O. Box 73
Earleville, MD 21919
costumesocietyamerica.com

National Association of Fine Artists
ArtNetwork
P.O. Box 1360
Nevada City, CA 95959
http://artmarketing.com

The National Association of Schools of Art and Design
11250 Roger Bacon Drive, Suite 21
Reston, VA 22090-5202
arts-accredit.org/nasad

National Assembly of State Arts Agencies
1029 Vermont Avenue NW, Second Floor
Washington, DC 20005
nasaa-arts.org

Professional Photographers Association
229 Peachtree Street NE, Suite 2200
Atlanta, GA 30303
ppa.com

The addresses for selected living history museums are provided below. In most cases, it is best to contact the personnel or employment office.

For a comprehensive list of links to websites of living history, agricultural, and open-air museums in the United States, Canada, and around the world go to alhfam.org/alhfam.links.

Colonial Williamsburg
Employment Office
P.O. Box 1776
Williamsburg, VA 23187
history.org/
Automated Job Line: (804) 220-7129.

Hancock Shaker Village
P.O. Box 927
Pittsfield, MA 01202-0927
hancockshakervillage.org

Plimoth Plantation
P.O. Box 1620
Plymouth, MA 02360
plimoth.org

Old Sturbridge Village
Director of Personnel
I Old Sturbridge Village Road
Sturbridge, MA 01566
osv.org

7

Path 3: Commercial Art

"Art is not what you see, but what you make others see."
—DEGAS

Commercial artists, also known as graphic artists and illustrators, put their artistic skills and vision at the service of commercial clients, such as major corporations, retail stores, and advertising, design, or publishing firms.

Their lot in life is much more secure than that of the studio artist, although a regular paycheck doesn't always guarantee the artistic freedom the former group enjoys.

Graphic artists, whether freelancers or employed by a firm, use a variety of print, electronic, and film media to create art that meets a client's needs.

Graphic artists are increasingly using computers, instead of the traditional tools such as pens, pencils, scissors, and color strips, to produce their work. Computers enable them to lay out and test various designs, formats, and colors before printing a final design.

Definition of the Career Path

Graphic artists perform different jobs depending on their area of expertise and the needs of their employer(s). Some work for only one employer; other graphic artists freelance and work for a variety of clients.

Graphic designers, who design on a two-dimensional level, may create packaging and promotional displays for a new product, the visual design of an annual report and other corporate literature, or a distinctive logo for a product or business. They also help with the layout and design of magazines, newspapers, journals, and other publications, and create graphics for television.

Illustrators paint or draw pictures for books, magazines, and other publications, films, and paper products, including greeting cards, calendars, wrapping paper, and stationery. Many do a variety of illustrations, while others specialize in a particular style.

Medical and scientific illustrators combine artistic skills with knowledge of the biological sciences. Medical illustrators create illustrations of human anatomy and surgical procedures. Scientific illustrators draw animals and plants. These are used in medical and scientific publications and in audiovisual presentations for teaching purposes. Medical illustrators also work for lawyers, producing exhibits for court cases, and for doctors.

Fashion artists draw illustrations of women's, men's, and children's clothing and accessories for newspapers, magazines, and other media.

Storyboards for TV commercials are also drawn by illustrators. Storyboards present TV commercials in a series of scenes similar to a comic strip, so an advertising agency and client (the company doing the advertising) can evaluate proposed commercials. Storyboards may also serve as guides to placement of actors and cameras and to other details during the production of commercials.

Cartoonists draw political, advertising, social, and sports cartoons. Some cartoonists work with others who create the idea or story and write the captions. Most cartoonists, however, have humorous, critical, or dramatic talents in addition to drawing skills.

Animators work in the motion picture and television industries. They draw by hand and use computers to create the large series of pictures which, when transferred to film or tape, form the animated cartoons seen in movies and on TV.

Art directors, also called visual journalists, read the material to be printed in periodicals, newspapers, and other printed media and decide how to visually present the information in an eye-catching, yet organized manner. They make decisions about which photographs or artwork to use and in general oversee production of the printed material.

Possible Employers

Many graphic artists work part-time as freelancers while continuing to hold a full-time job until they get established. Others have enough talent, perseverance, and confidence in their ability to start out freelancing full-time immediately after they graduate from art school. Many freelance part-time while still in school to gain experience and a portfolio of published work.

The freelance artist acquires a set of clients who regularly contract for work. Some successful freelancers are widely recognized for their skill in specialties such as children's book illustration, design, or magazine illustration.

These artists can earn high incomes and can pick and choose the type of work they do.

But more often than not, freelance careers take time to build. While making contacts and developing skills many find work in various organizations.

Still, other commercial artists prefer full-time employment over freelancing. They find work in the following settings.

Advertising Agencies and Design Firms

Persons hired in advertising agencies or graphic design studios often start with relatively routine work. While doing this work, however, they may observe and practice their skills on the side. Jobs can cover anything from direct-mail packages to catalog work, posters, and even include the television and motion picture industry.

Publishing Companies

Magazine, newspaper, and book publishers require the expertise of commercial artists for a wide range of duties including cover design, advertising layout, typesetting, and graphics.

Department Stores

Department stores, especially the larger chains, routinely produce catalogs, direct-mail packages, flyers, posters, and a variety of other advertising and promotional material. While small stores might send the work out to freelancers, large department stores often have fully staffed departments to handle the workload.

The Television and Motion Picture Industries

This is wide-open territory. Organizations such as Disney Corporation, for example, actively recruit new graduates right out of art schools starting with very attractive salaries. Opportunities are especially strong for those versed in computer graphics.

Other settings include manufacturing firms and the various agencies within the local, state, and federal governments.

Working Conditions

Graphic artists work in art and design studios located in office buildings or their own homes. Graphic artists employed by publishing companies and art and design studios generally work a standard forty-hour week. During busy periods, they may work overtime to meet deadlines.

Self-employed graphic artists can set their own hours, but may spend a lot of time and effort selling their services to potential customers or clients and establishing a reputation.

Peggy Peters: Freelance Illustrator

Peggy Peters teaches art at an alternative school in Texas. She also works as a freelance illustrator.

Peggy Peters discusses her career: "As my undergraduate degree was in fine arts, not graphic arts, it was difficult to make the transition to commercial art. Where I lived there were no schools with graphic arts majors and I didn't really know the field.

"Fortunately, I went for my master's at Syracuse University and earned my degree in illustration. The degree program was unique—only working illustrators were accepted. My group consisted of about sixteen people—illustrators from Alaska, Canada, California, England, Arizona, New York, and Virginia, among others. I gained a broad overview of the profession and the program was geared specifically to career development.

"At the present time, I am selling illustrations locally, working specifically with fine arts organizations, theaters, and an opera company. These organizations often use graphics for advertising—posters, illustrations for products to raise funds, cups, T-shirts, and so forth. In a year I plan to show my work to someone who does many of the Broadway show posters. I also did all the artwork for the 'World Flight Project' in which a local pilot, Linda Finch, duplicated the flight of Amelia Earhart in 1997. And I'm learning computer graphics. In the last ten years or so, three-fourths of all illustration and design jobs are done on computer, according to various trade magazines such as *Step-by-Step Graphics*."

Some Advice From Peggy Peters. "For a real jump start in your art career go to the best art school possible—Rhode Island School of Design, Chicago Art Institute, Syracuse University, CalArts, Savannah, and so forth. To the extent possible, you should become fluent in the use of computers before college. Learn PageMaker, QuarkXPress, Illustrator, Freehand, and some 3-D programs, and learn as much as you can before college.

"Target the type of design or illustration you want to do and study the careers of artists doing things you want to do. Write to a few artists to learn what they did. The days of big advertising design firms is gone. More and more people are working freelance and you don't have to be in New York City or Chicago to be successful anymore. In today's technology, illustrators are living and working everywhere.

"There are many different types of illustration/design careers. The best way to succeed is to find out what you really want to do, then go about finding out how to do it. For example, I love performing arts so my thesis for my M.A. was on Broadway poster illustrators. I found out how the top people in that field, Jim McMullan, Paul Davis, and so forth, structured their careers. This gave me some idea as to how I could do this myself and if my ideas were practical at all.

"The field changes rapidly so flexibility is another important consideration. For example, multimedia was the hot field a few years ago but it already is reaching a saturation point. Only about 5 percent of any multimedia product proves really successful and the investment to produce a product is very high."

Training and Qualifications

Graphic Arts

In the graphic arts field, demonstrated ability and appropriate training or other qualifications are needed for success. Evidence of appropriate talent and skill shown in the portfolio is an important factor used by art and design directors and others in deciding whether to hire or contract work out to an artist. The portfolio is a collection of handmade, computer-generated, or printed examples of the artist's best work. In theory, a person with a good portfolio but no training or experience could succeed in graphic arts. In reality, assembling a successful portfolio requires skills generally developed in a postsecondary art or design school program, such as a bachelor's degree program in fine art, graphic design, or visual communications.

Internships also provide excellent opportunities for artists and designers to develop and enhance their portfolios. Most programs in art and design also provide training in computer design techniques. This training is becoming increasingly important as a qualification for many jobs in commercial art.

Graphic artists may advance to assistant art director, art director, design director, and in some companies, creative director of an art or design department. Some may gain enough skill to succeed as a freelancer or may prefer to specialize in a particular area. Others decide to open their own businesses.

Medical Illustrator

The appropriate training and education for prospective medical illustrators is more specific. Medical illustrators must not only demonstrate artistic ability but also have a detailed knowledge of living organisms, surgical and medical procedures, and human (and sometimes animal) anatomy. A four-year bachelor's degree combining art and premedical courses is usually required, followed by a master's degree in medical illustration, a degree offered in only a few accredited schools in the United States.

In general, illustrators advance as their work circulates and as they establish a reputation for a particular style. The best illustrators continue to grow in ideas, and their work constantly evolves over time.

Strategies for Finding the Jobs

As in most any professional career, contacts and having a foot in the door at the type of organization for which you'd like to work are valuable assets. Internships are pathways to both.

The best strategy is to plan ahead. During your undergraduate or graduate studies, arrange for as many internships as you can squeeze in—either full-time during the summers or part-time during semesters.

Learning how an advertising agency, a public relations firm, or a TV studio functions will give you a broad overview and also help you build a successful portfolio.

If an internship gave you a foot in the door, a professional and creative portfolio can open that door all the way. In addition, find yourself a mentor, someone who can critique your portfolio and advise you on how best to proceed.

Career Outlook

Artists held about 147,000 jobs in 2000. More than half were self-employed. Of the artists who were not self-employed, many worked in motion picture, television, computer software, printing, publishing, and public relations firms. Some self-employed artists offer their services to advertising agencies, design firms, publishing houses, and other businesses.

The need for artists to illustrate and animate materials for magazines, journals, and other printed or electronic media will spur demand for illustrators and animators of all types. Growth in the entertainment industry, including cable and other pay television broadcasting and motion picture production and distribution, will provide new job opportunities for illustrators, cartoonists, and animators. Competition for most jobs, however, will be strong, because job opportunities are relatively few and the number of people interested in these positions usually exceeds the number of available openings. Employers should be able to choose from among the most qualified candidates.

Earnings

Median annual earnings of salaried multimedia artists and animators were $41,130 in 2000. The middle 50 percent earned between $30,700 and $54,040. The lowest 10 percent earned less than $23,740, and the highest 10 percent earned more than $70,560. Median annual earnings were $44,290 in computer and data processing services, the industry employing the largest numbers of salaried multimedia artists and animators.

Related Occupations

Many occupations in the advertising industry, such as account executive or creative director, are related to commercial and graphic art and design. Workers in other occupations that apply visual art skills are architects, display workers, floral designers, industrial designers, interior designers, landscape architects, and photographers.

The various printing occupations are also related to graphic art, as is the work of art and design teachers.

Professional Associations

American Institute of
    Graphic Arts
164 Fifth Avenue
New York, NY 10012
aiga.org

Cartoonists Association
113 University Place, Sixth Floor
New York, NY 10003
cartoonistsassociation.com

Graphic Artists Guild
90 John Street, Suite 403
New York, NY 10038-3202
gag.org

Industrial Designers Society of America
45195 Business Court, Suite 250
Dulles, VA 20166
idsa.org

The Society of Publication Designers
60 East 42nd Street, Suite 721
New York, NY 10165
spd.org

Students in high school or college who are interested in careers as illustrators should contact:

The National Association of Schools of Art and Design
11250 Roger Bacon Drive, Suite 21
Reston, VA 22090-5202
arts-accredit.org/nasad

The Society of Illustrators
128 East 63rd Street
New York, NY 10021-7392
societyillustrators.org

For information on careers in medical illustration, contact:

The Association of Medical Illustrators
2965 Flowers Road South, #105
Atlanta, GA 30341
medical-illustrators.org

For information on careers in scientific illustration, contact:

Guild of Natural Science Illustrators
P.O. Box 652, Ben Franklin Station
Washington, DC 20044-0652
gnsi.org

8

Path 4: Art History

Not surprisingly, most people who work in art museums are art lovers.
Often they are also art historians with a major in art history.

Art lovers keep museums functioning today, and in reality, they're the reason art museums started in the first place. Most of the famous art museums around the world acquired their exhibitions from private art collectors, whether through voluntary donations or as the result of political changes.

Historically, the principle of public control over art and art collections was firmly established in France during the Revolution, when the royal collection was nationalized in 1793 and opened to the public as the Louvre Museum.

In the late 1700s and early 1800s more and more privately owned collections became available for public view, such as those held by King Frederick William III of Prussia, leading to the establishment of the Kaiser Friedrich Museum in Berlin, and the Tsar's private art collection, forming the exhibits at the Hermitage Museum in Saint Petersburg, Russia.

The National Collection of Fine Arts in Washington, D.C., (renamed the National Museum of American Art in 1980) was the first federal collection of American art. Established in 1846 as part of the Smithsonian Institution, in 1906 it was designated a national gallery of art.

The word *museum* comes from the ancient Greek name for the temple of the Muses, the nine beings who were the patron goddesses of the arts in Greek mythology. The term was first used to refer to institutions of advanced learning and didn't take on its current meaning until the Renaissance, when the first great collections of art were formed in Italy. During the seventeenth and eighteenth centuries, art museums thrived throughout Europe. As in the Renaissance period, however, almost all collections were private, and public access was limited.

An exception to that was the collection of Sir Hans Sloane, which was bequeathed to Great Britain in 1753. It became the foundation for the British Museum, the first museum organized as a public institution.

In the late 1800s, several specialized museums were created in Europe, such as the Bavarian National Museum in Munich and the Museum of Ornamental Art in London, which was later renamed the Victoria and Albert Museum. The first museums to be set up as public institutions in the United States were the Museum of Fine Arts in Boston in 1870 and the Metropolitan Museum of Art in New York City in 1872. In 1879 the Art Institute of Chicago followed.

Definition of the Career Path

First, to understand the role of the art history major within art museums, it is important to understand the different types of museums and the roles they play.

Art museums are buildings where objects of aesthetic value are preserved and displayed. Art museums have a variety of functions including acquiring, conserving, and exhibiting works of art; providing art education for the general public; and conducting art historical research.

Since the beginning of the twentieth century, art museums have seen a number of trends, such as the expansion of large institutions and the creation of a horde of specialized museums, many of which are devoted to modern art. In contrast, a number of the world's largest museums have attempted recently to reduce their size and improve the quality of their collections. They have begun selling less important works of art to concentrate available funds on acquiring works of greater artistic merit or historical significance.

Art Museums

Art museums can be classified into two major categories: private museums, under the authority of a board of trustees composed of private citizens and a director chosen by the board, and public museums, administered directly by the national or local government.

In addition, art museums fall into two basic types: the general museum, presenting a broad range of works from early times to the present, and museums that specialize in one particular era, artist, region, or type of art.

In recent years, costs for building maintenance, staff, utilities, and insurance have escalated, while federal funding has decreased. How art museums support themselves has become a controversial issue. Once free to the public, many museums now charge admission. Membership subscriptions are aggressively sought as another major source of revenue. Most public museums now solicit donations from individuals and businesses and vie for corporate and government grants. These practices, while both legal and ethical, affect a museum's choices by forcing it to give precedence to those exhibitions and acquisitions that can be funded by outside sources.

In other words, the art you see displayed in a museum might not have been chosen for its aesthetic value alone, but for its ability to, at least in part, raise income. Exhibitions with mass appeal are most likely to find financial sponsorship; art that is less familiar to the general public is less likely to be funded.

This cold reality often creates a dilemma for a museum's director and acquisitions curator, but most museum professionals stand by their objectivity, frequently having to defend their independent position in spite of the preferences of patrons.

Natural History Museums

Dedicated to research, exhibition, and education in the natural sciences, natural history museums are also included in this career path. In addition to the expected collections of gems and jewels, fossils, meteorites, and animals from around the world displayed in lifelike settings, natural history museums also handle collections that include artifacts from ancient civilizations. Restoring and maintaining these artifacts fall to the responsibility of conservators, discussed later in this chapter.

Possible Job Titles

In the past, art museums functioned mainly as storehouses for objects, but in recent years their role has been greatly expanded. More and more large art museums try to serve the interests of the community in which they are located. In addition to exhibiting their own collections, many museums develop special "traveling" exhibitions that are loaned out to other institutions for display. They also conduct guided tours of their collections, publish catalogs and books, provide lectures and other educational programs to members of the general public, and offer art classes to students.

With all these varied roles, art museums can now offer a wealth of employment opportunities to job seekers.

Art Museum Curators

Curators in art museums are responsible for the preservation of the collection and for implementing its visual accessibility to the public. The curator is usually an art historian knowledgeable about the physical properties of handmade objects. While curators have a general background in the history of art, they usually specialize in a given area. Large museums with diversified collections employ several curators for the different departments such as American, European, modern, Oriental, primitive, decorative arts, or photography.

Curators oversee the collection and participate in obtaining new acquisitions. They also verify the authenticity of paintings or objects by researching its provenance, a document attesting to the work's previous owners and exhibitors.

The curator also supervises the installation of the museum's permanent collection. He or she determines the number of objects to be shown and decides when they'll be shown. Working with the exhibit designer, the curator also plans how objects or paintings will be displayed.

Erica Hirshler, Assitant Curator

The Museum of Fine Arts, Boston, has had its doors open for more than 130 years. The museum covers collections from all over the world with more than one million objects.

Erica Hirshler began work at the Museum of Fine Arts as a volunteer in 1983. Only four months later she was offered a paying, part-time job, which two years later developed into a full-time position as assistant curator. Erica earned her B.A. from Wellesley in art history and medieval studies in 1979, her M.A. in art history from Boston University in 1983, and a museum studies diploma the same year. In January of 1992 she earned her Ph.D. in art history, also from Boston University.

"We have two thousand paintings in the collection, and not every one has been studied for its historical significance. I study and work on the permanent collection, organize special exhibitions, do research, and write catalogs and art books, write label copy and brochure copy for exhibitions, and arrange for the display of different things in the galleries.

"I also handle a lot of correspondence with the general public. We get a lot of inquiries. They range from people who have a painting in their attic and don't know what it is to scholars who are working on projects at other institutions and need information on our collection. And I administer the loan requests for our department.

"Our paintings department has a European side and an American side. On the American side, where I work, there is a curator, an associate curator, and myself, assistant curator, and four research assistants and fellows of varying areas of specialization.

"Of course, it's every assistant curator's hope to move up the curatorial ladder. There's usually more money and prestige involved with a promotion. Often, to move ahead, a curator would have to be willing to change locations. But opportunities can be limited. Sometimes it's better to stay right where you are."

Erica explains, "We have one of the two best collections of American paintings in the country—the Metropolitan Museum of Art in New York City has the other—so, you balance the strength of being in an institution that values your field against some of the other things that might not be so positive. In other words, moving to a weaker collection to get a better title. It wouldn't be worth it.

"Going to a smaller museum with a smaller collection isn't necessarily a good career move unless you're interested in getting onto a director track. You could be a director at a small museum, then eventually a director at a bigger museum. But the more administrative your job becomes the less work you can do as a scholar."

Associate curators and/or curatorial assistants report directly to the curator and help with the varied tasks the profession demands.

Art and Object Conservators

Many people think that once something valuable gets into a museum, it's safe but, unfortunately, it decays on the museum's walls or shelves just as fast as it would decay on yours at home. Many different conditions contribute to that process: light, variations in humidity and temperature, pollutants, pests, and accidental damage. Conservators concern themselves with preventing that decay.

Art conservators, once known as art or painting restorers, preserve and restore damaged and faded paintings. They apply solvents and cleaning agents to clean the surfaces, reconstruct or retouch damaged areas, and apply preservatives to protect the paintings.

Object conservators help prevent deterioration through a number of steps:

1. By examining the object to determine its nature, properties, method of manufacture, and the causes of deterioration
2. Through scientific analysis and research on the objects to identify methods and materials
3. By documenting the condition of the object before, during, and after treatment, and by recording actual treatment methods
4. By taking preventive measures to minimize further damage by providing a controlled environment

5. Through treatment to stabilize objects or slow their deterioration
6. By restoring, when necessary, to bring an object closer to its original appearance

Being a conservator is a real team effort. Very often the conservator and curator call each other in and look under the microscope and discuss what they should do with a piece that's damaged—whether to leave it alone or just make it stable so it won't cause any further loss.

Conservators also deal with the exhibits department. The conservator tells them how they can build a mount for an object so that the object is supported. They provide much of the information that is displayed on labels and arrange for proper lighting levels so the colors don't fade.

Conservators also work closely with exhibit designers and curators when they're planning a new show or transporting objects. How an object is supported or wrapped so it can go to another museum without damage often falls into the conservator's realm.

And though working with visiting scholars often is part of a collection manager's job, conservators often instruct students about the correct way to handle an object.

Registrars

Registrars in art museums keep track of the location of all the various works of art in the museum's collection. Paintings and other art objects are often moved to different areas within a museum, or transported to other museums for exhibition. Because of this it is necessary to maintain accurate files. Registrars are also responsible for shipping objects and obtaining insurance.

Collections Manager

The collections manager supervises, numbers, catalogs, and stores the specimens within each division of the museum. An undergraduate degree in the area of the museum's specialization is the minimum requirement. An advanced degree in museum studies with a concentration in a specific discipline is recommended.

A collections manager must have knowledge of information management techniques and the ability to accurately identify objects within the museum's collection. Knowledge of security practices and environmental controls is also important.

Photographers

Many art museums keep a professional photographer on staff to provide photographic documentation of the various fine arts collections. The photogra-

THE REGISTRAR'S OFFICE, METROPOLITAN MUSEUM OF ART, NEW YORK CITY

While a small museum might have only one registrar, a large museum such as the Metropolitan Museum of Art in New York City needs a much bigger staff to cover all the responsibilities of an expansive and active collection.

Currently, in addition to the head registrar, the Metropolitan has four people handling exhibits, two working with outgoing museum loans, one dealing with loans to the museum and exams (items brought in for review), a storeroom manager, one conservator and one assistant to the conservator (in addition to the many conservators working in the conservation department), and four packers. The rankings for registrars at The Metropolitan Museum of Art are as follows:

Assistant registrar
Senior assistant registrar
Associate registrar
Head registrar

Aileen Chuk, Associate Registrar Metropolitan Museum of Art

Aileen Chuk worked for eleven years at the Museum of Modern Art in New York before coming to the Metropolitan in 1994. She has a bachelor's degree in art history from Fordham University in New York and currently serves a dual role as administrative manager and associate registrar.

As administrative manager she works directly with the head registrar taking care of all personnel issues and supervising the work of junior staff members.

Here Aileen tells us about her role as associate registrar.

"A registrar has a lot of functions, depending on the size of the institution. At the Metropolitan we have certain duties, mostly involving shipping of artworks. We take care of the packing, we make the transportation arrangements, arrange for couriers, take care of the insurance, and keep an archive of all of the works that are lent to the museum.

"Basically, a curator decides what he's going to have in a particular show and gives you a list of some two hundred objects. You have to make sure the loan agreements are signed and in place, make all the packing arrangements, contact the borrowers or the lenders to the museum, coordinate scheduling of shipments and courier arrangements, then make arrangements for the unpacking of those objects here. You coordinate with the conservation staff to check those works in concert with the curatorial staff."

continued

The Pros and Cons of Registrar Work

Although Aileen loves her work, as with most jobs, there are some downsides. "It takes a lot of personal time and frequently takes away from your family life. There's a great deal of overtime. Shipments come at two o'clock in the morning or they leave at five in the morning. Then there's a lot of traveling involved in escorting artworks. Sometimes you want to do it, sometimes you don't."

Salaries can be another downside. "Museum work can be extremely satisfying, but it's not a career suited for someone who is interested in making a lot of money," Aileen explains.

"All the negative issues aside, it's still very rewarding. You get to see a project from its inception to its completion. You also have the knowledge that you've been part of a very large effort to put on a show of major proportions."

What It Takes to Be a Registrar

"You need to be very detail-oriented and have good organizational skills. You're often working with two hundred artworks and have to remember all the details for all those artworks and what the lenders require. It's essential to have a good memory.

"Although I've seen people who've done this without an art background, I think it would be very helpful to have one. Generally, registrars have a strong interest in art—either they're artists themselves or they have painting skills or some artistic bent. Most have a bachelor's in art history. If you're really serious, you should pursue a preliminary degree in the arts so you have a familiarity with and understanding of the physical properties of artwork.

"Most of the job duties are learned on the job. There are also museum studies' programs that grant certificates. Some students choose that route after receiving their bachelor's degree. It's a good way to get your foot in the door. We get many interns from those programs—an internship is the best way to find out how a museum functions.

"There are a number of different specialties within the registrar's office and the more senior you get, the more complex work you're assigned. As you gain experience you tend to do exhibitions rather than museum loans or other departmental tasks."

pher would also oversee the photography of general museum events and activities. He or she would be responsible for studio and darkroom facilities and personnel issues for any assistants.

Many photographers are self-taught; others receive their training in a variety of ways—through traditional art schools, through university art and photography departments, and through apprenticeships.

A portfolio documenting your professional experience would be a requirement for employment. Photographers also find work in planetariums and other types of museums.

Educators

Almost all museums provide some sort of educational programming for the public. Educators and program developers design and arrange programs for the public. They explain the exhibitions, and conduct classes, workshops, lectures, and tours. They often offer outreach programs to the schools or local community in which they are located.

Educators usually possess a teaching certificate or have had teaching experience before they join a museum staff.

Tour Guide/Docent

Although most museums rely on volunteer help to act as tour guides and docents (the two job titles have essentially the same meaning), there are still a few spots for a paid professional. Most tour guides have a college degree in either education or the field of study the particular museum encompasses.

Training and Qualifications

With museums offering so many diverse careers, it stands to reason that avenues of training leading to these professions would be equally diverse. An art conservator would have a background different from a taxidermist, an educator's preparation would differ from an exhibit designer's.

In addition, different museums often look for different qualifications. Some prefer candidates to have an advanced degree or certificate in museology or museum studies. Others expect to hire professionals with strong academic concentrations in, for example, art history, history, or anthropology. Most are impressed with a combination of academic and hands-on training earned through internships or volunteer programs.

However, several skills and personal traits are common to all museum professionals. For a start, all museum workers need to have excellent interpersonal skills. Educators, tour guides, and exhibit designers present information to staff and visitors; directors and curators supervise staff and cultivate contacts with donors and other community members; interpreters, security guards, and museum gift shop staff constantly interact with visitors; museum support staff must deal with each other, and so on. The ability to get along with others and to work well as a team is a vital asset in museum work.

Of equal importance is the ability to communicate through the written word. Museums meet their missions with their collections of objects, but to do so, museum workers must have strong writing skills. Good written language skills show themselves in grant applications, exhibition catalogs, brochures, administrative and scholarly reports, training and educational materials, legal agreements, interpretive labeling for exhibits, object records, and much more.

Other personal characteristics and abilities are also crucial. Before pursuing formal training leading to a career in museum work, it would be a good idea to look at the following checklist and see how many of the items apply to you.

- Strong people skills
- Excellent oral and writing skills
- Manual dexterity
- A good imagination
- Creativity
- A healthy curiosity
- Resourcefulness
- Commitment to education
- Patience
- Flexibility
- Problem-solving ability
- Ability to handle multiple tasks
- An understanding of the mission of museums and how they go about achieving it
- Business skills
- Computer skills

The last item, computer skills, deserves additional mention. More and more museums are relying on computers to keep track of their collections, to design labels, and to produce catalogs and brochures, as well as other functions. The ease found in working with a variety of software programs can be only an asset to a prospective museum worker.

While many items on this list are natural skills, many can also be learned. How you proceed will depend upon your interests and circumstances. If you are clear from the start what avenue you wish to pursue, you can tailor-make a course of study for yourself at the university of your choosing. Courses you'll take or the degree toward which you'll work will depend in part on whether you are a new student or you are already a museum professional making a midcareer change.

Traditionally, new hirees to the field of museum work have completed a bachelor's and master's degree in academic disciplines appropriate to the intended career. Curators for art museums have studied art and art history; curators for natural history museums have studied biology, anthropology, archaeology, and so on. And while such a background still serves as the main foundation for successful museum work, for the last thirty years or so more and more people have explored university programs offering practical and theoretical training in the area of museum studies. Courses such as museum management, curatorship, fundraising, exhibition development, and law and museums offer a more specific approach to the work at hand. This, coupled with a broad background in liberal arts or specialization in an academic discipline, provides the museum professional with a knowledge base better designed to serve the needs of the museum.

Whatever your course of study, these days most museums require an upper level degree, either in an academic discipline or in museum studies, museum science, or museology. Also required is an intensive internship or record of long-term volunteer work.

What follows are three possible tracks with which a student can proceed to prepare for a career in museums:

Track One
- Bachelor's degree in general museum studies, museology, or museum science
- Master's degree or doctorate in a specific academic discipline
- Internship arranged through the university or directly with a museum in a particular field

Track Two
- Bachelor's degree in liberal arts or a specific academic discipline
- Master's degree or certificate in museum studies, museology, or museum science
- Internship arranged through the university or directly with a museum in a particular field

Track Three
For the museum professional changing careers or upgrading skills:

- Master's degree or certificate in museum studies
- Non–credit-bearing certificate in museum studies (short term course)

The internship is considered the most crucial practical learning experience and is generally a requirement in all programs. The internship can run from ten weeks to a year with varying time commitments per week.

Training for Curators

Employment as a curator generally requires graduate education and substantial practical or work experience. Many curators work in museums while completing their formal education, to gain the hands-on experience that many employers seek when hiring.

In most museums, a master's degree in an appropriate discipline of the museum's specialty, for example, art, history, archaeology, or museum studies, is required for employment as a curator. Many employers prefer a doctoral degree, particularly for curators in natural history or science museums. In small museums, curatorial positions may be available to individuals with a bachelor's degree.

For some positions, an internship of full-time museum work supplemented by courses in museum practices is needed.

Training for Museum Technicians

Museum technicians generally need a bachelor's degree in an appropriate discipline of the museum's specialty, museum studies training, or previous museum work experience, particularly in exhibit design.

Technician positions often serve as a stepping-stone for individuals interested in curatorial work. With the exception of small museums, a master's degree is needed for advancement.

Training for Conservators

Conservators are a group of highly trained professionals who have gone through a number of steps to gain their expertise. Training programs are few, and as a result, are very competitive.

According to the American Institute for Conservation of Historic and Artistic Works, the qualities a conservator must have are:

- Appreciation and respect for cultural property of all kinds—their historic and sociological significance, their aesthetic qualities, and the technology of their production
- Aptitude for scientific and technical subjects
- Patience for meticulous and tedious work
- Good manual dexterity and color vision
- Intelligence and sensitivity for making sound judgments
- Ability to communicate effectively

During the course of a training program student conservators are exposed to work with a variety of materials, before going on to specialize in a particular area. They learn skills to prevent the deterioration of paintings, paper and books, fiber, textiles, ceramics, wood, furniture, and other objects. There are even conservators in architectural conservation and library and archives conservation.

Training most traditionally is gained through a graduate academic program, which takes from two to four years. Apprenticeships or internships are a vital part of training and are usually taken during the final year of study. Some programs might offer internships that run concurrently with classes.

Admission requirements for the various graduate programs differ, but all of the programs require academic prerequisites, including courses in chemistry, art history, studio art, anthropology, and archaeology.

Some programs prefer candidates to already have a strong background in conservation, which can be gained through undergraduate apprenticeships and field work in private, regional, or institutional conservation laboratories. A personal interview is also usually a requirement of the application process. A candidate's portfolio must demonstrate manual dexterity as well as familiarity with materials and techniques.

Careful planning at the undergraduate level will help improve your chances of acceptance into a graduate program, but because acceptance is very competitive, it is not unusual to have to repeat the application process. Before reapplying, however, it is a good idea to enhance your standing by undertaking additional studies or fieldwork. Many programs, on request, will review your résumé and suggest avenues for further study.

Conservation Degree and Internship Training Programs. The names and addresses of the conservation degree and internship training programs currently active in North America are listed at the end of this chapter. Contact those that interest you for their specific admission requirements.

Strategies for Finding the Jobs

Although formal, academic training is vital to your résumé, hands-on experience is of equal importance. Not only does it provide a host of significant skills, but it also allows the career explorer to make an informed decision about the suitability of museum work. A person who starts with a term of volunteer work, even before beginning a college program, will have a better idea of what career options museums have to offer and whether these options are right for him or her.

Many museums rely heavily on volunteer energy and can place volunteers in almost every museum department, from tour guide and gift shop sales to assisting curators and exhibit designers. The easiest way to volunteer your time is to call a museum and ask to speak to the volunteer coordinator. He or she will work with you to match your interests with the museum's needs.

Volunteer programs are usually flexible about the number of hours and days per week they expect from their volunteers.

Most academic museum studies programs require an internship before a degree or certificate can be awarded. In addition, many museums have their own internship programs that are offered to full-time students as well as recent graduates. You can check with your university department first to see what arrangements they traditionally make. If the burden is on you to arrange an internship, either during your academic program or after you've graduated, contact the museum's internship coordinator. If the museum has no formal internship program, talk first to a museum staff member to determine where there might be a need. Then, you can write a proposal incorporating your interests in a department where help will be appreciated.

Internships can be either paid or unpaid and are usually a more formal arrangement than volunteering. The number of hours and weeks will be structured and the intern might be expected to complete a specific project during his or her time there. Often, college credit can be given.

The American Association of Museums has published a resource report called "Standards and Guidelines for Museum Internships." It covers what museums expect from their interns and what interns can and should expect from the museum.

Later, when it comes time to job hunt, a successful internship or stint of volunteer work can open the door at the training institution or at other museums.

Career Outlook

Competition for jobs as curators and museum technicians is expected to be keen as qualified applicants outnumber job openings. Graduates with highly specialized training, such as master's degrees in both library science and history, with a concentration in archives or records management, and extensive computer skills should have the best opportunities for jobs as archivists. A curator job is attractive to many people, and many applicants have the necessary training and subject knowledge; but there are only a few openings. Consequently, candidates may have to work part time, as an intern, or even as a volunteer assistant curator or research associate after completing their formal education. Substantial work experience in collection management, exhibit design, or restoration, as well as database management skills, will be necessary for permanent status. Job opportunities for curators should be best in art and history museums, since these are the largest employers in the museum industry.

The job outlook for conservators may be more favorable, particularly for graduates of conservation programs. However, competition is stiff for the limited number of openings in these programs, and applicants need a technical background. Students who qualify and successfully complete the program, have knowledge of a foreign language, and are willing to relocate, will have an advantage over less qualified candidates.

Employment of curators and museum technicians is expected to increase about as fast as the average for all occupations through 2010. Jobs are expected to grow as public and private organizations emphasize establishing archives and organizing records and information, and as public interest in science, art, history, and technology increases. Although overall museum attendance is increasing, public interest in smaller, specialized museums with unique collections is expected to increase faster. However, museums and other cultural institutions are often subject to funding cuts during recessions or periods of budget tightening, reducing demand for archivists and curators. Although the rate of turnover among archivists and curators is relatively low, the need to replace workers who leave the occupation or stop working will create some additional job openings.

Earnings

Median annual earnings of curators and museum technicians in 2000 were $31,460 in museums and art galleries. Median annual earnings of curators and museum technicians in 2000 in all settings were $33,080. The middle 50 percent earned between $24,740 and $45,490. The lowest 10 percent earned less than $19,200, and the highest 10 percent earned more than $61,490.

Earnings vary considerably by type and size of employer and often by specialty. Average salaries in the federal government, for example, are usually higher than those in religious organizations. Salaries of curators in large, well-funded museums can be several times higher than those in small ones.

The average annual salary for museum curators in the federal government in nonsupervisory, supervisory, and managerial positions was $64,616;

museum specialists and technicians, $44,711; and archives technicians, $33,934.

Professional Associations

The following list of associations can be used as a valuable resource guide in locating additional information about specific careers. Many of the organizations publish newsletters listing job and internship opportunities, and others offer employment services to members. A quick look at the names of the various organizations will give you an idea of how large the scope is that museums cover. Most maintain websites; phone numbers are listed for those that don't.

African-American Museum Association
P.O. Box 427
Wilberforce, OH 45384
artnoir.com/aaam

American Arts Alliance
805 15th Street NW, Suite 500
Washington, DC 20005
artswire.org/~aaa

American Association for Museum Volunteers
c/o Sarah Christian
Denver Museum of Nature and Science
2001 Colorado Boulevard
Denver, CO 80205-5798
(303) 370-6363

American Association of Museums
1575 Eye Street NW, Suite 400
Washington, DC 20005
aam-us.org

American Federation of Arts
41 East 65th Street
New York, NY 10021
afaweb.org

American Institute for Conservation of Historic and Artistic Works
1717 K Street NW, Suite 301
Washington, DC 20006
http://aic.stanford.edu

Archives of American Art
Administrative Office
Smithsonian Institution
8th and G Streets NW
Washington, DC 20560
aaa.si.edu

Art Libraries Society of North America
329 March Road, Suite 232
Box 11
Kanata, ON K2K 2E1
Canada
arlisna.org

Association of Art Historians
Cowcross Court
70 Cowcross Street
Clerkenwell
London EC1 M6EJ
United Kingdom
http://scorpio.gold.ac.uk/aah

Association for Art History
Henry Radford Hope School of Fine Arts
Fine Arts 124
Indiana University
Bloomington, IN 47405
indiana.edu/~aah

Association of Art Museum Directors
Head Office
41 East 65th Street
New York, NY 10021
aamd.org

Association of Art Museum Directors
Washington Office
1319 F Street NW, Suite 201
Washington, DC 20004
aamd.org

Association of Children's Museums
1300 L Street NW, Suite 975
Washington, DC 20005
childrensmuseums.org

**Association of College and University
   Museums and Galleries**
Brigid Brink, ACUMG Coordinator
Sam Noble Oklahoma Museum of Natural History
The University of Oklahoma
2401 Chautauqua Avenue
Norman, OK 73072
snomnh.ou.edu/acumg/index

Association for Volunteer Administration
P.O. Box 32092
Richmond, VA 23294
avaintl.org

Canadian Museums Association
280 Metcalfe Street, Suite 400
Ottawa, ON K2P 1R7
Canada
museums.ca

Independent Curators Incorporated
799 Broadway, Suite 205
New York, NY 10003
(212) 254-8200

**Institute of Museum and
   Library Services**
1100 Pennsylvania Avenue NW
Washington, DC 20506
imls.gov

Internship Program, Office of Museum Programs
Smithsonian Institution
Arts & Industries Building, Room 2235
Washington, DC 20560
si.edu/ofg/internopp.htm

International Association of Museum Facility Administrators
P.O. Box 1505
Washington, DC 20013-1505
iamfa.org

International Council of Museums
ICOM Secretariat
Maison de l'UNESCO
1 rue Miollis
75732 Paris Cedex 15
France
icom.org

International Museum Theatre Alliance
c/o Wildlife Theater
Central Park Zoo
830 Fifth Avenue
New York, NY 10021
mos.org/learn_more/imtal.html

Museum Education Roundtable
621 Pennsylvania Avenue SE
Washington, DC 20003
http://users.erols.com/merorg

Regional Museum Associations
Association of Midwest Museums
P.O. Box 11940
St. Louis, MO 63112-0040
midwestmuseums.org

Mid-Atlantic Association of Museums
1 East Chase Street, Suite 1124
Baltimore, MD 21202
midatlanticmuseums.org

Mountain-Plains Museum Association
7110 West David Drive
Littleton, CO 80128
frontier.net/~mpma/mpmaindex.htm

New England Museum Association
Boston National Historical Park
Charleston Navy Yard
Boston, MA 02129
nemanet.org

Southeastern Museums Conference
P.O. Box 3494
Baton Rouge, LA 70821
semcdirect.net

Western Museums Association
655 Thirteenth Street,
   Suite 301
Oakland, CA 94612
westmuse.org

Degree and Internship Training Programs
The following symbols designate the level of training the following conservation training programs offer:

   U—Undergraduate
   G—Graduate
   P—Postgraduate
   I—Internships
   C—Courses

Art Conservation Department (G)
Buffalo State College
230 Rockwell Hall
1300 Elmwood Avenue
Buffalo, NY 14222
buffalostate.edu/depts/artconservation

Art Conservation Center at the University of Denver (formerly the Rocky Mountain Regional Conservation Center)
2420 South University Boulevard
Denver, CO 80208
du.edu/accdu

Art Conservation Department (U,G,P)
University of Delaware and Henry Francis du Pont
    Winterthur Museum
303 Old College
University of Delaware
Newark, DE 19716
http://seurat.art.udel.edu

Art Conservation Programme (G)
Queens University
Kingston, ON K7L 3N6
Canada
queensu.ca/artconv/artcon

Campbell Center for Historic Preservation Studies (C)
203 East Seminary Street
Mt. Carroll, IL 61053
campbellcenter.org

Canadian Conservation Institute (G,P,I)
Training and Information Division
Department of Communications
1030 Innes Road
Ottawa, ON K1A 0C8
Canada
cci-icc.gc.ca

Columbia University (G)
Graduate School of Architecture, Planning, and Preservation
400 Avery Hall
New York, NY 10027
columbia.edu

Conservation Center, Institute of Fine Arts (G)
New York University
14 East 78th Street
New York, NY 10021
nyu.edu/gsas/dept/fineart/html/cns.htm

Johns Hopkins University (P)
(Ph.D. in materials science with a concentration in conservation science,
    sponsored by the Smithsonian Conservation Analytical Laboratory)
Department of Materials Science & Engineering
Room 102, Maryland Building
Baltimore, MD 21218
jhu.edu

Getty Conservation Institute (C)
4503 Glencoe Avenue
Marina del Rey, CA 90292
getty.edu/gci

Straus Center for Conservation (G,P,I)
Harvard University Art Museums
32 Quincy Street
Cambridge, MA 02138-3383
artmuseums.harvard.edu/straus/index

University of Pennsylvania (G)
Graduate Program in Historic Preservation
Architectural Conservation Laboratory
115 Meyerson Hall
Philadelphia, PA 19104-6311
upenn.edu

University of Texas at Austin (G)
Graduate School of Library & Information Science
Preservation & Conservation Education Programs for Libraries and
    Archives
Austin, TX 78712-1276
utexas.edu

9

Path 5: Art Galleries

"A man paints with his brains and not with his hands."
—MICHELANGELO

Art galleries are generally privately owned and are similar to specialized museums in which the collection is restricted to the works of a single artist. Art galleries can also focus on a specific historical period, category of art, or geographical region.

Art galleries operate differently from art museums. While the museum depends on membership and grants to support itself, an art gallery must earn its keep by selling works of art to the public.

Who owns art galleries? Art lovers, for one. You can't open and operate a gallery without having a strong love as well as a deep understanding for the world of art.

Who works in art galleries? More art lovers. But the list doesn't end there. Included also are art aficionados with a flair for selling and studio artists earning extra money to make ends meet—in a setting where they will be in constant contact with other artists and art lovers.

Definition of the Career Path

Some art galleries are small with only one or two employees in addition to the director/owner. Large galleries, especially those in New York, maintain a staff of ten, fifteen, twenty people, most of whom would carry the title of assistant director.

The following are typical jobs found in art galleries:

• **Director/Owner.** The owner of an art gallery is responsible for every aspect of running the gallery, from selecting which artists to exhibit, to designing the layout of the show, hanging the artwork, promoting the show and the gallery, and selling to clients.

• **Assistant Director.** A large gallery could have ten or so assistant directors. These individuals work directly with the owner, representing the gallery and reflecting the owner's taste. Assistant directors work with customers, or clients, as they are frequently called, discussing the artwork and making sales.

• **Packager/Maintenance Personnel.** Most large galleries have "backroom staff," personnel responsible for packaging purchased pieces of art for shipping and maintenance workers who, under the direction of the director or an assistant director, hang the paintings in designated positions. In many cases packagers or maintenance personnel are artists who take a menial job in a gallery to allow them to continue to be able to paint and still be involved in some level in the art world. It's also a good way for a future assistant director to get his or her foot in the door. It puts you in contact with the art arena, allowing you an opportunity to learn. You'll hear why they're showing someone and how they're exhibiting someone and what is being done to publicize the show. It's always worthwhile to know every aspect of the business and these so-called "menial" jobs are very important.

• **Framer.** Most small galleries farm out their work to frame shops, but the larger galleries often have a framer on staff who is skilled in cutting mats for prints and cutting frames for canvases. However, most artists deliver their work to galleries already framed, so the need for professional framers hired directly by a gallery is small.

• **Receptionist.** Many large galleries, especially those in New York, hire receptionists to greet customers and answer questions over the phone. They must be knowledgeable about the artwork shown and be able to intelligently discuss different aspects of the work. Most receptionists have a degree in art; many use the position as a stepping-stone to assistant director.

Hear what it's like firsthand owning your own art gallery:

Matthew Carone, Gallery Owner

Matthew Carone is the owner of the Carone Gallery, a prestigious establishment in Fort Lauderdale, Florida. He handles mainly contemporary art, American, some European and some Latin-American paintings and sculpture. He is also an established painter himself and often is invited to show his work at other galleries.

"I acquire artwork in a couple of ways. I'm now in a position where I can be very selective about the number of artists who would like to show with me. After you have a track record and you've established yourself, you get to that plateau where the artist knows of your reputation and wants to be in your stable of artists.

"But when you're starting out, you have to trust your own taste and be on the lookout for undiscovered talent. Establish yourself as a serious gallery. I happened to do it by way of master graphics. I got involved in the early years with original prints, not reproductions, but very serious Picassos, very important Cézanne and Matisse prints.

"Many of the sources for these prints happened to be in Europe, which allowed me to go there every two or three months. The most important dealers in Europe met once a month to discuss what was happening in the art world, what was new, what was fake, that sort of thing. As it turned out, I had discovered a Picasso fake and got a lot of mileage and publicity through that.

"I'm color blind, but I became value sensitive. I can see the value of a color, the lightness or darkness, more so than a person with normal color vision. The ink used for this one Picasso was called an ivory black, which is the blackest of blacks, but I knew that the originals had a warmer black. On the basis of that I knew there was something wrong, so I went to Paris and showed it to a very important Picasso dealer. He said to me, 'Mr. Carone, if you had showed me this print framed, under glass, I would have said it was okay, but you're right, this is a fake.' This led me to Picasso's biggest dealer, but my biggest mistake was when he said we must show this to Picasso—I should have insisted that I go along with that print, but I didn't do that.

"They sent it to him and Picasso did send it back to me with a 'faux' (fake) with a line through it. But Picasso signed it, meaning 'Picasso says faux' so it then achieved some value. Anything he put his name to had value and the faux print became an interesting thing to see. A prominent international auction house said that the print was very good, so whoever the artist was, he had a lot of talent. The fake was terrific. The FBI, of course, got involved with this; they had an idea who he was, but it was never pursued because it's very difficult to prove. They never found out.

"This event came at that time of my life when I was getting involved seriously and it gave me a new level of importance. Everybody started banging on my door wanting me to look at their Picassos. Now, over the years I've developed a clientele that comes to me for particulars.

"I always felt that you never sell a painting, you sell yourself first. That's really a barometer for selling. And if I really love something, it's the easiest thing in the world for me to sell because, if my clients pick up on my enthusiasm, they're sold. The consumer is, in most cases, not really sure of their taste and if what they like is good. My loyal clients automatically become an extension of what I feel about art."

The Day-to-Day Running of an Art Gallery

"In addition to client contact, I talk with artists who want to show with me. They send me slides that they want me to see. I never refuse to talk to them. Part of the fun is looking at all the art and deciding who you want to show. The artists might be wonderful, but then you also have to evaluate whether or not you'll be able to sell their works. Each space on the wall costs you X amount of money. You have to make your expenses and every inch of wall space must pay for itself.

"You also have to concern yourself with the installation of a particular show and where a painting belongs in relation to another painting. Hanging the art is something you need to have a feel for. For instance, I have ten thousand square feet, five thousand feet on each level, so we have a big, expansive space to hang many different kinds of art. And it's very important to be able to hang an artist next to someone he's compatible with. You don't want any conflicts in image. You wouldn't want to put an ethereal kind of painting next to a very guttural abstract. You could destroy that very sensitive painting if it's within the view of something incompatible. You learn this on the job and through discussion. There's no one book that can describe this, it's a gut feeling.

"While you have a show up, you're always anticipating and planning for the next show. I usually do a show for three weeks, then give myself a week off between shows. I don't usually do more than four shows a season. Then, after the shows, you bring out your own inventory, things you own outright that you have accumulated over the years.

"It's been the most wonderful life for me. I can't tell you how great it's been. First of all I'm a painter, I play the violin, and I use my gallery for concerts. I come to work thinking I'm coming home. I'm going to where I want to be. I love the artists, I love selling important stuff, and I love people responding to my enthusiasm. It's been glorious. I'm a very lucky guy— I absolutely love what I do."

Strategies for Success

This advice comes directly from Matthew Carone:

"It's sometimes difficult to even get a job interview with the larger galleries. I never refuse to talk to anyone who is aspiring to get into the business—they can come in and pick my brain. Someone interested in pursuing a career in an art gallery should go talk to an established art gallery owner to get a feel for the business.

"Contacts are great to have before you start out. Even before you get your feet wet you should go to museums and speak to curators and directors. And, of course, go to the better galleries—make an appointment to have a dialogue, an informational interview. If they're honest, they'll paint a true picture for you of what it's all about. If you want to chance it, then it's up to you, but at least you've given yourself that edge.

"And if you want to open your own gallery, first decide what you want to sell and promote. Being idealistic about it is one way to go, if you have faith in a particular artist but you know his work would be difficult to sell. Great art is not always palatable on your initial response. Even Picasso, before he became famous, was laughed at by most of the people in the world. You have to be brave and have a conviction about the art, and that, of course, comes out of a love for it. You have to be sincere.

"Rental of the space is the main factor. I would always look for a space in the best location, even though it might be more expensive. If you can be in a cultural area, near a museum, that would be ideal. To look for a very inexpensive space off the beaten track is not the way to go.

"Think of the cost of a year's rent. Other expenses are minimal. You have blank walls painted white, track lighting, a desk, and a little storeroom. There are advertising costs, brochures, announcements, your insurance, and utilities and any salaries you'll have to pay. That's the beginning.

"Then you have to get a stable of artists who would reflect your taste, who would help establish your image as a serious gallery.

"In a craft gallery it might be easier to sell your inventory, but I wouldn't advise it as a way to get into serious art. It could be financially successful; people love crafts. Success on that level is easier than going for fine arts. More people will respond to a pot than a painting and you'll have a bigger audience.

"The tragedy of the fine arts is that it caters to only 3 percent of the population. Now that could be quite a bit, if you're in a cultural area, but that 3 percent is distributed among the arts in general, music and arts, so if you want to hone in on just a segment of that, on just painting or sculpture, there's not that much out there. You're in a minority arena. It's a risky business. However, when something happens to have a magical combination—it's good and the public responds to it—that's paradise!"

Training and Qualifications

The background most gallery owners and assistant directors need is to be able to talk about art on an historic level: what happened fifty years ago, one hundred years ago, the evolution of art, and so forth. Knowing the "language of art" makes it easier to sell current artists' work in terms of what their past influences were.

To prepare for a job, a degree in art would be beneficial, whether art history or applied arts. But it can be done without it. You're also evaluated on your presence and how articulate and extroverted you are without being pushy—you don't ever want to be pushy. That mentality turns people off.

Sales skills can be learned, but you must have a sincerity about the work.

Earnings

Most galleries work on a 50/50 percentage basis with the artist. But if it's a very popular artist, the gallery might take only 30 percent. The cost of the artwork could range from $2,000 for a small wooden mask to $10,000 or more for paintings. Matthew Carone says: "I've sold art for $43,000, and that's not the most expensive I've shown. With an artist who has a following, the more popular they are, the bigger the attraction they are, the better for you."

Professional Associations

Art Dealers Association of America, Inc.
575 Madison Avenue
New York, NY 10022
artdealers.org

Association of College and University Museums and Galleries
Brigid Brink, ACUMG Coordinator
Sam Noble Oklahoma Museum of Natural History
The University of Oklahoma
2401 Chautauqua Avenue
Norman, OK 73072
snomnh.ou.edu/acumg/index

The Visual Arts and Galleries Association
The Old Village School, Witcham, Ely
Cambridgeshire CB6 2LQ
United Kingdom
vaga.co.uk/cgi-bin/vaga2/vaga2

Index